BEATING DEPRESSION

THE JOURNEY TO HOPE

Maga Jackson-Triche, M.D., M.S.H.S.

Kenneth B. Wells, M.D., M.P.H.

Katherine Minnium, M.P.H.

M<small>C</small>G<small>RAW</small>-H<small>ILL</small>

NEW YORK   CHICAGO   SAN FRANCISCO.   LISBON
LONDON   MADRID   MEXICO CITY   MILAN   NEW DELHI
SAN JUAN   SEOUL   SINGAPORE   SYDNEY   TORONTO

McGraw-Hill

*A Division of The **McGraw·Hill** Companies*

1 2 3 4 5 6 7 8 9 0   DOC/DOC   0 9 8 7 6 5 4 3 2

ISBN 0-07-137627-5

This book was set in New Times Roman by MM Design 2000, Inc.

Printed and bound by R.R. Donnelley & Sons.

McGraw-Hill books are available at special quantity discounts to use as premiums and sales promotions, or for use in corporate training programs. For more information, please write to the Director of Special Sales, Professional Publishing, McGraw-Hill, Two Penn Plaza, New York, NY 10121-2298. Or contact your local bookstore.

This book is printed on recycled, acid-free paper
containing a minimum of 50% recycled, de-inked fiber.

To my mother, Essie,
who always told me how much she loved me;
to my patient and thoughtful husband, David;
and to my funny and energetic sons, James and Henry.
MJ-T

To the Partners in Care study team and the participating patients,
practices, and clinicians for allowing us to learn more
about treating depression; to my parents for their faith in me;
and to my wife, Christina Benson and my sons
Matthew and Michael, for filling my life with their passions,
talents, and understanding.
KBW

To my friends and family.
KM

CONTENTS

INTRODUCTION

Clinical Depression is a medical condition that changes the way a person feels, thinks, and acts. It affects a person's mood, behavior, thoughts and physical condition. Things that used to be easy or enjoyable, such as spending time with family or friends, reading a good book, or going to the movies, take more effort. Even basic things like eating and sleeping become a problem. For some, even sex seems uninteresting.

Many people suffering with Clinical Depression don't realize that they have a medical illness. They feel sick, or incredibly sad. They feel hopeless because they don't know how to get better, and nothing seems to help.

This book is for those of you who have days, weeks, and even years of feeling downhearted and sad. This book is also for those who care about you, your family, friends and colleagues. Our goal is to help you recognize the signs and symptoms of Clinical Depression and give you the good news that there are treatments that work. There is hope and there is help.

Although science has made great strides in developing antidepressant medications, good treatment involves more than just getting a pill. And, medications are not the only treatments that work. We discuss the latest research findings and give you information about how to work with clinicians to get the care you need. We also describe ways that you can help yourself.

Many do not realize that depression is a common illness. Each year, in the United States alone, almost 17 million people suffer with Clinical Depression. Young or old, rich or poor, male or female; anyone can become clinically depressed. Your race, ethnicity, or religious affiliation does not matter. Studies show that approximately 1 in 10 men and 1 in 5 women have Clinical Depression at some point during their lifetime.

Clinical Depression is probably best described as an imbalance in the chemicals that stabilize mood. There are chemicals in the brain that help regulate how you feel. These substances are responsible for keeping your mood in balance. Scientists are making important advances in learning exactly how these substances regulate mood and behavior. When the levels of certain chemicals are too low, mood can become depressed. Although scientists aren't clear about what causes levels to decrease, it is becoming clear that certain circumstances and situations can increase the likelihood of someone becoming depressed. The death of a loved one, catastrophic events such as losing a job, having a severe financial setback, getting a serious medical illness are all situations in which a depression can occur.

Clinical Depression runs in some families. Just as with other medical disorders, there are cases where depression appears to be an inherited illness. If someone in your family, especially someone in your immediate family (parents, grandparents, brothers, sisters), suffers with Clinical Depression, your risk of developing Clinical Depression increases.

The pain and suffering of Clinical Depression affects not only the person with the disorder. It affects everyone who cares about them. This impact can extend to the workplace because the symptoms of depression make it particularly difficult to function normally at work. It is common for the depressed to find that their work performance deteriorates as their symptoms worsen. The depressed use more sick days. Clinical Depression can be a very disabling illness. Depression is expected to become the second leading cause of disability worldwide by 2010.

Because of increased healthcare costs and decreased income from lost work, depression can be a very expensive disorder. The same is true for society's costs. In 1990, depression and other Mood Disorders cost the United States more than $40 billion dollars, mostly from lost productivity.

Many of the findings that we present in this book come from the RAND Partners in Care research study. This clinical study, started in the mid-1990s, looked at ways to improve the quality of depression care in primary care medical practices. Most people with depression go to their family doctor first. This study focused on helping these doctors recognize and treat depressive symptoms. The study also trained nurse care coordinators and added resources for offering psychotherapy.

As you read through the chapters you'll notice quotations from study participants. These are real people who were kind enough to share their individual experiences with you. We hope that reading their words will help you understand that you are not alone.

It is our sincere wish that this book will benefit you. Life may be painful, now, but it doesn't have to stay that way. As we say throughout the book, there is hope.

LETTER TO THE READER

THE STORY AND FINDINGS OF PARTNERS IN CARE

Being a researcher is like being both a detective and a witness. You try to understand a problem and bring it to light, and then you look at what you've found and contain it inside yourself, sometimes for years, until it's shared publicly in a scientific article. Sometimes what you "witness" is quite upsetting, as is often the case with studies of depression's impact on people. Sometimes researchers try to learn what would happen if things were different—such as if depression care were better. There are two main ways of trying to learn about that in medicine, either by observing different situations (like people receiving different kinds of care) or creating new situations (like an intervention to improve care) and watching what happens.

As a researcher, I spent over ten years being a "witness" to depression's effects on people.[1] I learned that depression's impact on quality of life and day to day functioning was comparable to or greater than the impact of most other major illnesses in medicine, such as diabetes. After publishing those findings, I received letters from depressed people in the general public, telling me that they felt understood and were relieved that the story of the broad impact of depression had been made public in terms that others might understand. I learned through the study that some people sought care from a specialist like a psychiatrist or psychologist and others sought care from their general medical doctor. Still others sought no care at all. This concerned me, because I knew from my own training that primary care doctors had many other medical problems to attend to when they saw depressed patients and might not notice the depression. I learned that despite availability of effective treatments, few (perhaps 20 to 30%) among those visiting primary care clinicians received treatments for depression that met standards for good or "appropriate" care in published national standards or guidelines.

This problem is not unique to depression. A recent report from the Institute of Medicine documents that many people with major physical health problems do not receive effective care for those problems and there are many unnecessary errors in medical treatments. This is considered a widespread "system problem" in medicine.[2]

I am a psychiatrist as well as a researcher. While as a researcher I can be a witness, as a clinician, I want to try to do something about the problems I observe. When I realized after ten years of research that lots of Americans with depression were suffering over long periods of time, and that this suffering was affecting their ability to live well, feel pleasure, work, and have friends, I looked for a chance to find out how to improve things. I felt we already knew that good treatments make depressed patients recover. What I wanted to find out was whether feasible programs to support good decisions by doctors and patients in real community health care practices could improve the chances that the average depressed patient got good care, and whether this was enough of a difference in the practice of medicine to make a real difference in lives of depressed people in the practices.

Fortunately, we were funded to answer these questions by the Agency for Healthcare Quality and Research, the main federal agency that evaluates the quality of American healthcare. We obtained additional funding to complete the study from the MacArthur Foundation and the National Institute of Mental Health.

Our team of investigators worked together for about a year to study the best available treatments for depression, national practice guidelines, and approaches to improve care for depression developed by leading researchers (such as Wayne Katon in Seattle, and therapies developed by Ricardo Munoz at the San Francisco General Hospital's Depression Clinic). Under the direction of Lisa Rubenstein, an internist, our team put together a comprehensive "toolkit" or set of strategies for practices to use to educate patients and doctors and provide them with resources (like training programs in effective therapy and medication management) for good depression care.

The study then recruited large primary care practices around the United States (Southern California, Southern Colorado, San Antonio, TX, Columbia, MD, Twin Cities, MN) to participate in the study. Those practices agreed to provide some of their own resources to help protect doctors' time to participate and to hire staff to help with the interventions. Teams of clinicians (primary care, specialists, nursing) within the practices came to a centralized training, to learn how to use the toolkit to improve care within their practices. This included, for example, learning how to educate clinicians and patients about the principles of good care. Then we also trained special staff within the practices—therapists and nurses—to provide assessments, coordinate care, and provide therapy and consultation on medications.

After this training, the practices used the toolkits, with their trained study staff, to try to improve care. They trained their primary care doctors, and routed patients to the nurses, therapists, and consultants trained to help coordinate their care and to provide treatments. With these special resources (called "quality improvement programs"), doctors and patients made their own decisions about treatment. They could even decide not to use the study interventions if they did not want to, and they could decide not to start any treatment if that's what the patient and doctor thought was best.

To evaluate what happened as a result of the programs, the study compared similar depressed patients in clinics, called intervention clinics, that used these intervention programs and patients from clinics, called usual care clinics, that did not have these programs. The practices' clinics were randomly assigned to having one of the interventions or not, so this was a type of randomized trial of the intervention programs. The usual care clinics did receive written copies of the national guidelines for treating depression, but not other intervention.

After identifying the patients in both intervention and usual care clinics, the study collected data from the providers, practices, and patients over two years. That is, as researchers we "watched" what happened. In all, 181 primary care doctors participated in 42 clinics. Over 23,000 adults were screened for depression in these practices, and 1356 with probable depression were enrolled. Roughly two-thirds of these were in intervention clinics and one-third were in usual care clinics.

Although a lot of planning went into the study and the development of the practice interventions, as the "world turns" these would not be considered very intensive interventions. That's because no one was assigned to treatment, and no one (doctors or patients) were told what to do with any particular case.

What did this kind of program do for patients with depression? Let's break this question down into a series of specific questions.

Was the intervention program feasible for the practices? We found that, yes, most practices could implement the basic features of the "quality improvement" intervention programs. The nurses who provided case management for medication had some of the most complex new responsibilities. We found that for less structured parts of the intervention, like the number of follow-up contacts with patients about their medication, there was a lot of variation across practices, and actually most patients did not get all the recommended follow-up visits under the intervention model.

Did more patients who got the study programs get good care for depression? Yes, more depressed patients got good care by national standards if they were in a clinic with an intervention program, rather than in a usual care clinic. The percentage with good care at six months was about 45% in the intervention clinics, compared to about 35% in the usual care clinics. That is, with this kind of "information support" program, the good care rate jumped about 10 percentage points—not a huge change, but enough to see if, step-by-step, improved depression care improves patients' lives.

Did more patients recover under the special programs? Yes, by about 10 percentage points, more patients recovered from a serious depression at six months and at one year under the special programs, compared to usual care. Actually, we also found that for some of the special programs (those that particularly focused on improving availability of an effective psychotherapy for depression), improvements in quality of life lasted well into a second year of follow-up, relative to the patients in a "usual care" clinic with no special program. This is a very long period of time to show improvement for patients, especially for such a "light" intervention with flexible decisions by patients and doctors.

What about employment and functioning? Here were some big surprises. We found that not only did depression improve, but patients in the clinics with special programs were more likely to remain employed or to enter the workforce at six months, 12 months and 18 months. After one year, at least 5% more of the special program patients were working, compared to the usual care program patients. You may have noticed in the newspapers that the national unemployment rate is about (and sometimes below) 5%. That means that the programs reduced unemployment of depressed patients by about the magnitude of the national unemployment rate! That seems like a very large benefit of the programs. Over two years, the intervention patients had about one month more of employment than the usual care patients, all from getting better information and support for getting good depression care, without being forced into any decisions about care!

While those findings look like good evidence of effectiveness, when talking about healthcare, people usually ask whether the benefits were worth the costs.

What was the value or "bang for the buck?" We looked at that question, too, and found that the total costs to society of providing the program over two years was about $500 per patient; and that led to roughly an additional month of employment (worth more than $500 to many people) and the equivalent of a full month of feeling completely well (spread out over two years of follow-up). We put it to you, does that $500 (to society) seem worth it? That value is well within the range of benefits expected per dollar spent for many types of medical treatments that are in place routinely today. That suggests that we are acting, if you look at our healthcare decisions in other areas, as though this is a good value.[3]

Did people from all walks of society benefit? We didn't say this before, but this study had large samples of minority patients (especially people of Latino background), and many people who were poor or had low income or wealth. Thus, the good news about the study findings, particularly in terms of clinical improvement, applies across diverse ethnic groups.

Perhaps the biggest surprise in the finding is the improvement in employment, and the improvement in personal economic development that is likely to follow, from having better opportunities to get good depression care. In many ways, this finding is part of why we thought it was important to try to get the message of this study—that people can improve their lives by actively seeking and obtaining the care they need for depression—to the public.

Remember that to help people get their life back, in the study, we spent a year figuring out how to help their practices improve their ability to give good care! That shows how hard it can be to change the healthcare system and change the behavior of doctors and patients. But really, there was no "rocket science" or high technology involved in helping people. There were no fancy computer systems (though in the future there probably will be), and the doctors provided no untried or experimental treatments. It was a matter of providing explanations and information and connecting people to people to make and support good decisions.

We decided to write this book to share with people how they might get the help they need to get their lives back, based on these various findings and our experiences with this study. We've tried to include what we think would interest or help the public from those years of work.

For me as study director, it's sort of full circle. Based on treating patients personally, I became interested in what was keeping many people with depression from getting good treatment. As a researcher I became a witness, and spent ten years documenting and publishing what I saw. Of course, I was not alone in this witnessing, and observed what my fine colleagues were finding in other studies, including the techniques they were developing to improve the situation. Then I got a lot of help in mounting a study to see what would happen when doctors and patients had better information and resources for developing partnerships for good depression care. Then it was back to being a witness, and watching what happened. And the results surprised and encouraged me. I saw that the good will of many doctors and patients went into efforts to improve care, and saw the quality of care take a step (but only a step) forward. But even so, the ripple effects for patients were surprising to me—the improvement in lives, the reduced suffering, and, the improvement in their ability to hold down jobs. These benefits were obtained at a modest cost, as healthcare interventions go.

Now, with this book, the information is back to you, the public, the consumers, the sufferers and the loved ones of those with depression. That's the completion of the circle. We can't promise you that you'll be able to get the care you need, but we hope that from this book you'll be more hopeful and knowledgeable and have some tools to help you get the care you need. My colleagues and I are most grateful for the opportunity to write this book, and hope it is of some use to those who suffer from Clinical Depression.

Sincerely,

Kenneth B. Wells, M.D., M.P.H.
Principal Investigator of Partners in Care

[1] Wells, K., Sturm, R., Sherbourne, C., and Meredith, L. *Caring for Depression.* Cambridge: Harvard University Press, 1996.

[2] Kohn, Linda T., Corrigan, Janet M., and Molla S. Donaldson, editors. Committee on Quality of Health Care in America, Institute of Medicine. *To Err Is Human: Building a Safer Health System.* Washington, DC: National Academy Press, 2000.

[3] Schoenbaum, M., Unützer, J., Sherbourne, C., Duan, N., Rubenstein, L., Miranda, J., Meredith, L., Carney, M. and Wells, K. Cost-effectiveness of practice-initiated quality improvement for depression: Results of a randomized controlled trial. *Journal of the American Medical Association* 286(11) (2001):1325–30.

JUST THE "BLUES," OR SOMETHING MORE SERIOUS?

"Depression has meant I had to face the world with a view apart from most."

From time to time everyone has days when they feel unhappy, times when they feel down and discouraged. In fact, a person who denies ever having moments of feeling downhearted or "blue" wouldn't be believed. Because everyone has moments when they feel in low spirits, it can be hard to recognize when sad feelings are just the "blues" of everyday life, or when these feelings signal serious illness.

Janet Johnson* was someone faced with this problem. Janet was a woman admired by everyone she met. She seemed to "have it all." She was a wife, a mother of two small daughters, and managed her own real estate business. She taught Sunday school and led an energetic Girl Scout troop. Last year, anyone asking her how she felt would receive the answer that despite being extremely busy, she really enjoyed her life.

Nonetheless, a few months after her 35th birthday, something changed. Over a period of several weeks she began to have more

* Not a real person—a composite.

and more days when she felt "down" and "out of sorts." There was no particular event that she could pinpoint as the cause. Her business was doing well, despite a slow real estate market, and her family was fine. Nothing out of the ordinary had happened. Still, she had trouble falling asleep and felt tired all the time.

Things weren't going well with her Girl Scout troop either. She no longer enjoyed their outings or other activities. Friends commented that she looked tired and suggested that she was working too hard.

Janet realized that she was having trouble concentrating when an important client found several mistakes on paperwork she had completed and intended to submit to a local bank. The client was furious and threatened to fire her. After discussing the situation with her husband, she decided to decrease her office hours.

Cutting back didn't help, however. Janet continued to feel unhappy, and after weeks of being down, she had little hope of ever feeling better.

THE TIME FACTOR

Symptoms are early warning signs. They are the body's way of saying that something's not quite right. One of the first and most important ways to distinguish between "the blues" and Clinical Depression is the length of time that symptoms last. In Clinical Depression, symptoms are present for most of the day, nearly every day for at least two weeks.[1]

Because Janet felt low for several weeks, and because she had almost no days of feeling good, Janet was probably suffering from more than just a bad case of "the blues." Her trouble sleeping and concentrating, combined with constant low spirits, may mean that she was suffering from Clinical Depression.

Table 1.1 lists those areas of life affected by depression.

Table 1.1 Ten things to know about clinical depression

Clinical Depression Can Affect:

1. Sleep
2. Appetite
3. Thinking
4. Ability to work
5. Hope
6. Enjoyment
7. Sex
8. Relationships with family and friends
9. Energy level
10. One's will to live

WHAT ARE THE SYMPTOMS OF CLINICAL DEPRESSION?

People with Clinical Depression experience symptoms that last for weeks and can stretch into months, even years. Again, the single most important warning sign is the length of time that symptoms last. Symptoms must be present most of the day, almost every day, for at least two weeks.

There are many different symptoms associated with Clinical Depression. It is important to understand, however, that Clinical Depression doesn't affect everyone in the same way. Not everyone experiences the same group of symptoms and symptoms can vary in intensity. Symptoms can be mild, moderate or severe. They can range from those that cause minor personal discomfort to those that cause severe distress, disrupting the ability to function at home and at work. A general rule of thumb is that the more symptoms a person has, the greater the odds of his having Clinical Depression.

The next section lists and describes the kinds of feelings that can occur during an episode of Clinical Depression.

A person with Clinical Depression usually experiences several of these symptoms.

SYMPTOMS OF DEPRESSION

1. Weeks of Feeling or Looking Sad and Down-Hearted

People with this symptom may not have the ability to talk about how sad they feel. Friends and family easily pick up on their unhappiness by looking at their faces, however. They cry easily and are much more tearful than usual. When asked why, they can't give a reason.

Becoming sad or upset is common when someone suffers a severe setback, such as losing a job, family troubles, relationship difficulties, or money problems. Because feeling unhappy in bad circumstances is understandable, some people have a tendency to ignore or make light of an enduring sad mood. They attribute their misery to their situation in life.

Those who are *not* clinically depressed feel better as the bad situation improves. They feel uplifted when something good happens. With Clinical Depression, the mood remains down despite good news.

For some people the sadness comes without warning. In fact, things may be going well. There is a type of Clinical Depression that happens to new mothers a few weeks after giving birth. In the midst of such a happy event, their overwhelming sadness and distress confuses them and their families. There are more details about this and other types of depression in Chapter 2.

2. Feeling "Numb" or "Empty"

Instead of feeling sad or blue, some say that they feel "nothing." These feelings can be very frightening. Those who have them experience a deep emptiness or numbness inside. Hearing good news or bad news, nothing makes a difference. Nothing makes them feel better. Some describe it as feeling like a "zombie" or a robot. They just go through the motions of living without being engaged or enthusiastic about anything.

4

3. Losing Interest in Things that Used to be Enjoyable

"I felt myself slipping further and further away from my friends and family. I stopped dating. Had no interest in sex. I let myself go. I used to ride my bike 50 miles every other day. Now nothing."

Clinical Depression causes sufferers to lose interest in activities that they used to find enjoyable. Hobbies like fishing, bowling, reading, needlework, shopping, and sports no longer seem fun or even worth the effort. People who are clinically depressed lose interest both in the activity and the ability to experience pleasure while doing the activity. Some even lose their desire for and interest in sex.

4. Trouble Concentrating, Thinking, Remembering, or Making Decisions

In Clinical Depression, people have trouble concentrating and paying attention to details. They lose their focus. One of the first signs is a problem with reading or listening. Thinking becomes a slow, dreary process. This can particularly be a problem for the elderly, especially those who already have problems with their memory.

These symptoms can have a negative impact on a person's ability to do their work. Those who can't concentrate have trouble following simple directions and can't complete assignments on time.

Losing the ability to concentrate doesn't only impact those who work at jobs that require a lot of reading. This symptom can have serious consequences for those in hazardous occupations where safety is a chief concern. Any job that requires a high level of vigilance and attention can be affected.

Memory problems are common in people who have lost the ability to focus and pay attention. Remembering important things becomes a problem. Most people can recall the experience of walking into a room to get something, then forgetting what it was. This kind of thing is common.

The memory problems of Clinical Depression are different. They are more severe. People may forget important dates or the name of a family friend. Fortunately, in depression, these symptoms are temporary. They resolve when the depressive episode ends.

5. Trouble Sleeping

"When I first start getting sick it usually starts with me not being able to sleep. I get really depressed and paranoid."

One of the most common symptoms of depression is trouble falling and staying asleep. It is very common for depressed people to complain that they lie in bed long hours, eyes wide awake, unable to fall asleep. Then, after managing to fall asleep, they toss and turn, waking after only a few hours. Then they can't get back to sleep. They lie in bed, exhausted, until it's time to get up. Even those who easily fall asleep complain of waking much earlier than usual. They then spend the rest of the day tired. Sleeplessness compounds problems of low energy and fatigue.

A less common but equally troubling problem is that of sleeping *too* much. People with this symptom have trouble staying awake. Despite sleeping unusually long hours, they fall asleep during the day. They have trouble getting up in the morning. Even though they sleep a lot, they never feel rested.

6. Loss of Energy and Motivation

". . . I get in a slump with feelings of worthlessness or a sense of 'I just don't care anymore' where it is a chore to put on my shoes when I get up. . . a great deal of effort just to get dressed in the morning."

Feeling tired is common when faced with a busy, hectic life. Fatigue can be a healthy signal that the body needs rest. The level of fatigue experienced by the depressed is different from the kind of fatigue that comes from working too hard, however. It is deeper, more intense, and in many cases, disabling.

Sometimes, family and friends notice that a person who has always taken pride in her appearance no longer seems interested in how she looks. In the past she was careful about her makeup and very particular about her clothes. Now she doesn't seem to notice that her clothes are wrinkled, even dirty. When asked about the change, she says that she's too tired to care.

Someone, who is usually well organized, who gets work done quickly, starts missing deadlines. He complains that even though he's sleeping a lot, he just doesn't have the energy that he once had. He comes to work late and calls in sick a lot.

The exhaustion of depression, added to problems with attention and concentration, makes performing normal, daily activities difficult. Tasks that seem simple for others are difficult, almost impossible, for someone who is severely depressed. Taking a shower or getting dressed in the morning is more than some can manage. They lose their will to do things that require even minimal effort. They have trouble with simple tasks because they just don't have enough energy, and resting or taking time off doesn't make the daily feelings of tiredness go away.

7. Change in Appetite and Eating Habits

"Three months later I went from 200 pounds to 107. My doctors, who I still see, were extremely worried about me. I didn't care if I lived or died and I cried all the time."

Clinical Depression affects appetite. Many with Clinical Depression lose interest in food. They eat less and miss meals without becoming concerned. They lose significant amounts of weight without trying. They can lose as much as ten pounds over the period of a few weeks. Sometimes they only notice when their clothes no longer fit.

Although loss of appetite is the more common symptom, there are those who eat much more than usual. They can't seem to control their eating and gain weight. They describe this experience as eating more, but enjoying it less, or not at all.

8. More Irritable, "Edgy," Nervous or Agitated

"I also get confused and I do not know what I do. I get to the point where I cannot think and I do not know what happens, what I do, or what I say! I get all of my family members worried. I get worries about my kids and all of their problems. All of my thoughts race through my head. And I get scared! I get scared because I don't know what goes on!"

Besides the other mood changes, the depressed can notice that they feel more irritable than usual. Things that they previously tolerated now upset them. They feel nervous or "on edge" most of the time. Loved ones and friends notice that they are cranky or angry, and easily lose their temper.

9. Feeling Worthless or Guilty

"You feel so worthless and you're in so much pain you just want the pain to be over. All you want is to be happy and worthwhile. To be strong, to carry on, and do things, to help others and not feel so lousy."

Self-esteem is very low in people suffering with Clinical Depression. People feel that they are worthless, that they have nothing to contribute to themselves or others. They feel that their life is unimportant and has no meaning.

Some begin to blame themselves for things that were beyond their control. In depression, they can feel extremely guilty about a minor thing that happened a long time ago. It can be a thing that they haven't thought about in years. Some feel guilty about being depressed. They lose their perspective. Without any evidence, they believe that they have done something wrong.

The guilt contributes to the feelings of worthlessness, and until their mood returns to normal, reassurance doesn't work.

10. Feeling Hopeless, Including Thoughts of Death or Suicide

"Everything in life seems meaningless and frustrating. I am having trouble finding a happy place for me. . . . I try to keep things in perspective and keep busy, but sometimes I feel like I am in a boxing match and being knocked down three times."

One of the most troubling and frightening symptoms is hopelessness. Many with depression feel deep despair. They're afraid that things will never get better. Some become convinced that nothing will ever help and begin to long for death. They feel that they would be better off dead. In the worst case, they make plans to kill themselves.

11. Frequent Body Aches and Pains or, Digestive Problems

"After a couple of months, things escalated. . . . I had headaches, heart palpitations, diarrhea, and dizziness. I could no longer function at my job and had to take a sick leave."

Sometimes physical complaints are the most prominent symptoms of a depression. Body aches and pains, bowel irregularity, digestive problems are common. These symptoms can be confusing, and can lead people to conclude that their problems are only physical.

Medical evaluations, however, usually don't find an illness that explains the severity of symptoms.

12. Isolating from Family and Friends

"What I experienced is a lot of loneliness and not feeling part of the family or group. I have felt like I was walking in a daze and not really here. I have felt very tired and I just wanted to end it all. Just leave this world. I felt like everything that could go wrong did go wrong and it was my fault. I did not want to participate in any activity. I really felt very alone and empty. 'Life is not fair.'"

Many depression sufferers have trouble being around others. This includes family members and close friends. They isolate themselves and don't want to participate in family and other group activities. Although they don't enjoy being alone, they don't have the energy to socialize.

13. Abnormal Thoughts and Experiences

"After a couple of months things escalated. More stress, more pressure. It was too much. I felt like I was losing my mind. I became afraid of everything from going to work to having dinner out with a friend."

When depression becomes severe, the sufferer may begin to have strange thoughts and experiences. Imagining that voices are speaking to them or saying critical things about them; feeling that someone is out to do them harm without any evidence; believing that something is terribly wrong with their body despite being physically healthy are some of the terrifying symptoms that occur in severe depression.

14. Changes in Physical Activity

"Depression really started to overtake me. I started to slow down, not that I wanted to—my physical body made me. It was very hard for me to admit

*I was having problems I couldn't work out for myself. The depression be-
came worse. I was feeling worthless. I couldn't do as much before, and
no matter how hard I tried to push myself and forget about things, the
pain was always there physically and mentally. . . . No one understood—
especially my family—why I couldn't be 'Super Mom' and 'Super Wife'
anymore."*

Some depressed people find that it takes them much longer to do
their daily tasks at home and at work. Depression can feel like living in "slow motion." Activities such as getting dressed, eating,
and walking take much longer than usual. Even with a great deal
of effort, people who are depressed can't speed up or move at a
normal pace. This can be very frustrating and confusing.

Feeling restless, jittery, or jumpy are other physical symptoms
seen in Clinical Depression. Many depressed people have trouble
sitting still and complain of feeling anxious and nervous most of
the time. Regardless of what's happening around them, and
despite reassurance from family and friends, nothing can calm
them.

If you have any of these symptoms, and you experience them
almost every day for at least two weeks, you may be suffering
from Clinical Depression. Clinical Depression and "the blues"
may seem very similar, but they are not the same. "The blues" feel
bad, but they are not as serious as having depression.

Depression can affect all aspects of a person's life. The difference between "the blues" and a depressive episode is similar to
the difference between getting a cold and having pneumonia. Both
depression and pneumonia need treatment.

Table 1.2 lists the key symptoms of depression. Reviewing this
list will help you determine whether you have symptoms that
match those of Clinical Depression.

Table 1.2 Things I'm experiencing

(Place a check by the symptoms you are experiencing or have experienced in the past few months, then indicate how much that symptom is affecting you.)

✔	Key Symptoms and Problems	Does this symptom affect you a little of the time, some of the time or a lot of the time?		
	Feeling sad or "empty"	____A little	___Some	___A lot
	Loss of interest in things that used to be enjoyable like sex, sports, reading, or listening to music	____A little	___Some	___A lot
	Trouble concentrating, thinking, remembering, or making decisions	____A little	___Some	___A lot
	Trouble sleeping or sleeping too much	____A little	___Some	___A lot
	Loss of energy or feeling tired	____A little	___Some	___A lot
	Loss of appetite or eating too much	____A little	___Some	___A lot
	Losing weight or gaining weight without trying	____A little	___Some	___A lot
	Crying or feeling like crying	____A little	___Some	___A lot
	Feeling irritable or "on edge"	____A little	___Some	___A lot
	Feeling worthless or guilty	____A little	___Some	___A lot
	Feeling hopeless or negative	____A little	___Some	___A lot
	Thinking about death, including thoughts about suicide	____A little	___Some	___A lot
	Frequent headaches, body aches, and pains	____A little	___Some	___A lot
	Stomach and digestive trouble with bowel irregularity	____A little	___Some	___A lot
	Other symptoms:	____A little	___Some	___A lot
		____A little	___Some	___A lot
		____A little	___Some	___A lot

MYTHS ABOUT DEPRESSION

There are several myths and misunderstandings about Clinical Depression. The fact that most people have limited access to good information is, to a large extent, responsible. This adds to the stigma that plagues those with emotional problems and prevents many from seeking care. The next section reviews some of the common myths and briefly explains why they are not true.

1. Myth: "It's my own fault. I must have done something wrong."

Reality: Clinical Depression is a medical disorder caused by a complex combination of genetic, biological, social, and environmental factors. The intense pain, suffering, and sadness of this disorder are no one's fault.

2. Myth: "These feelings are a sign of personal weakness or a character flaw."

Reality: There are some people with depression who think that their illness is a sign of personal weakness. This is truly unfortunate, because they don't realize that their suffering is the result of a medical illness.

This impression gets reinforced when people tell them that they're just whining or exaggerating. This implies that, if they were stronger, their problems would go away. The emotional and physical effects of depression can't be overcome by trying to "tough it out."

3. Myth: "Religious people shouldn't get depressed."

Reality: No one would say that religious people shouldn't get arthritis or diabetes. Clinical Depression is no different than other medical conditions. Anyone can develop a medical disorder and anyone can become depressed.

4. Myth: "It's shameful to have emotional problems."

Reality: Some of the shame associated with depression comes from the belief that people can control how they feel. If this were true, no one would ever have a bad day. Just as there is no shame in having high blood pressure, there is no shame in having Clinical Depression.

5. Myth: "I just have to struggle through this, because no one can help me."

Reality: The wonderful news about Clinical Depression is that there are many successful treatments. There is help, but finding it is not always easy. This book can serve as a guide.

6. Myth: "People with lots of money and friends don't get depressed."

Reality: Neither wealth nor fame is a protection against depression. As you'll read in the following chapters, anyone--regardless of income or social status—can become depressed.

7. Myth: "Ending my life is the only solution."

Reality: People become suicidal when they see no way out and give up on the possibility of ever feeling better. There is a saying: "suicide is a permanent solution to a temporary problem." People with depression are not doomed to a life of relentless misery. There is help and there is hope.

8. Myth: "Children and teenagers don't get depressed."

Reality: Although depression is less common in the young, it does happen. However, it is often more easily missed because people don't expect children to experience depressive symptoms. Children and teenagers also become depressed. The symptoms, though, are somewhat different in these age groups. Chapter 6 discusses some of the special issues related to depression in the young.

9. Myth: "I shouldn't tell anyone about these feelings."

Reality: Keeping quiet is one of the worst things to do. People with depressive symptoms need help. It is important to get a good assessment and talk to a qualified professional. Family and loved ones can provide support, but full recovery requires more. Chapter 4 explores ways to get the help that they need.

10. Myth: "The poor don't have the luxury of getting depressed."

Reality: Making health a priority is difficult when money is scarce. It is important to know that people living in poverty may be at greater risk for developing depression. The ongoing stress of managing life with limited resources can make them more vulnerable to this disorder.

CHAPTER 2

WHAT IS DEPRESSION AND WHAT CAUSES IT?

Depression is not a new illness. History shows us that people have suffered with depression as long as humans have walked the earth. Since earliest times, healers have recorded symptoms identical to those that we see today in Clinical Depression. Writings from ancient Egypt, Rome, Arabia, and Asia document that physicians recognized it as a unique illness. Hippocrates, a Greek physician who lived around 400 B.C., named it "melancholia" for the overwhelming sadness of those who endured it.

Throughout history, depression has affected people of all nationalities, colors, and creeds, including the famous. Napoleon, Caesar, Karl Marx, and Vincent van Gogh are a few of those well known to history who had mood problems that would today be diagnosed as depressive illness. Current celebrities who have talked publicly about having depression include Rosie O'Donnell,[1] Rosemary Clooney,[2] Tipper Gore,[3] Janet Jackson,[4] and Angelina Jolie.[5]

WHAT IS "MOOD"?

Mood is a word that describes your state of mind. It expresses your feelings and emotions. Happy, unhappy, cheerful, irritable, nervous, and relaxed are some of the words used when talking about mood.

Besides describing how you feel inside, mood also expresses your outlook on life. In other words, your mood communicates how you feel about yourself and the world around you.

We most often recognize a person's mood by the expression on his or her face. But we can also tell a lot about how someone feels by the way they walk and hold their body. A woman who slowly shuffles along with her head hung down and a frown on her face is probably not very happy.

There is a wide range of moods that can be described as "normal." As you know, your mood can change from day to day, even moment to moment, depending on the kinds of things that happen. When doctors talk about normal or stable mood, what they mean is that a person feels basically okay. There is a general sense that the emotions are steady and not out of control.

This does *not* mean that someone with stable mood always feels happy. Instead, a person with normal mood, despite having the occasional down day, generally feels confident that they can handle most things without too much difficulty.

Disturbed mood is a hallmark of Clinical Depression. It belongs to the diagnostic category known as "Mood Disorders." We do not yet know the exact cause of Clinical Depression. However, we do recognize that some of the same things that cause severe emotional distress, such as experiencing bad or catastrophic events, are associated with an increased risk of developing Clinical Depression.

CHEMICAL CHANGES IN DEPRESSION

"I think at times in your life certain situations or circumstances can help you through your depression as they can also add to it. The truth is it is always there, that chemical imbalance in the brain that threatens your life every day, even if [you're] not aware of it or no one around you is."

Although the direct cause of Clinical Depression is not yet known, there is a rapidly growing field of scientific information exploring the chemical changes that take place in the brain during an episode of depression. Not too long ago, researchers discovered chemicals in the brain that stabilize mood. These substances influence, and may even determine, how a person feels, thinks, and acts. Most of this information comes from research into the kinds of chemicals that relieve depressive symptoms.

These chemicals belong to a category of substances that carry messages between brain cells. The term used for these substances is *neurotransmitters*. Current research indicates that when levels of certain neurotransmitters are too high or too low, mood becomes disturbed. *Norepinephrine* and *serotonin* are two of the most important neurotransmitters thought to regulate mood.

So far, scientists do not understand what directly causes neurotransmitter levels to change. In some ways it is like the old question, "Which came first—the chicken or the egg?" Events inside and outside the body interact so closely that it is nearly impossible to determine the actual sequence of chemical events that leads to a depressive episode.

Current thinking suggests that neurotransmitter levels change in response to many things. A number of investigators speculate that the same factors associated with an increased risk of depression also cause chemical changes in the brain. The theory is that these chemical changes then, produce the typical symptoms of depression.

CONDITIONS AND CIRCUMSTANCES THAT CAN INCREASE THE CHANCES OF BECOMING DEPRESSED

Living in terrible circumstances, experiencing bad or catastrophic events, abuse of drugs and alcohol all increase the chance of developing mood problems. Likewise, some medical illnesses and some prescription medications bring on symptoms of Clinical Depression.

This section will discuss some of the common factors associated with increased risk for Clinical Depression. It's important to state, however, that although most people with depression experience one or more of these conditions, some become depressed without having any known risks. A person living in good circumstances can become depressed.

1. Family History

"... I believe my father masked his depression and shyness with his alcohol. ... I believe depression can really be a hereditary disease, but also certain situations can make it a part of your life. You see, I know; I fought it all my life along with alcoholism. That's why it was so hard for me to [accept] I had the disease."

Some families have many members who suffer with some form of depressive illness. Because of this finding, researchers believe that there is a genetic component to some forms of depression. To say that a disease is genetic is *not* to say that everyone in a particular family will become depressed. What it means is that the risk increases. If someone in your immediate family has a history of Clinical Depression, your risk increases. Immediate family includes your parents, grandparents, brothers and sisters, and your children.

2. Significant Losses or Bad Events

Every life is touched by events that cause severe pain and distress. People don't always respond in the same way, even though the circumstances are the same or similar. Each individual has a unique way of responding to stress.

Even though each person responds in their own way, it is clear that those who suffer significant losses, or whose life circumstances are very stressful, are more likely to develop Clinical Depression.

Some common events that can trigger depression include: the death of a loved one—especially a spouse, parent or child—forced separation from the people you care about; serious illness in you or a loved one; divorce and other marital or relationship troubles; financial problems, and losing a job. A setback doesn't have to be dramatic to cause a Clinical Depression. Depending on the circumstances, changing jobs or having a child go away to college can feel like a significant loss.

When a loved one dies there is always a period of mourning. This is a time of great personal sadness and emptiness. Grieving people experience some of the same symptoms as those with Clinical Depression. With time, however, the sadness gradually improves. After about a year, most people adjust and go on with their lives.

Nonetheless, this kind of loss can trigger depression. When this happens, the symptoms worsen instead of improving with time. Some people deteriorate to the point where they can't manage at home or at work.

Table 2.1 can help you think through whether you have recently experienced events that had an adverse effect on you.

Table 2.1 Life events I have experienced: During the past 12 months, did any of the following things happen to you?

Someone close to me died.	YES	NO
I had a serious argument with someone who lives at my home.	YES	NO
I had a serious problem with a close friend, relative, or neighbor not living at home.	YES	NO
I separated, divorced or ended an engagement or relationship.	YES	NO
I had arguments or other difficulties with people at work.	YES	NO

Table 2.1 Life events I have experienced: During the past 12 months, did any of the following things happen to you? (Cont.)

Someone moved out of my home.	YES	NO
I was laid off or fired from work.	YES	NO
I had a serious injury or illness.	YES	NO
I had minor financial problems.	YES	NO
I had a major financial crisis.	YES	NO
Someone close to me had a sudden serious illness or injury.	YES	NO
I, or someone important to me, had problems because of discrimination based on age, gender, race, ethnicity or immigration status.	YES	NO
I lost my home.	YES	NO
Other:	YES	NO

3. Medical Illness

"My depression was caused by being down due to physical injuries to my body. . . that required surgeries and rehabilitation programs for a couple of years. . . . To me, it meant I was less than a man at times when I thought of not being able to help around the home with physical tasks and duties."

"I believe my depression is a result of Systemic Lupus Erythematosus and its treatment. I have been on steroids for 25 years. I have also been inside avoiding sunlight for 25 years. . . . I became very fearful and angry. At the same time, I was expected to drastically change my lifestyle."

Some medical illnesses, especially diseases of the nerves and brain, are associated with an increased risk of Clinical Depression. It is common for people who suffer with Parkinson's disease, multiple sclerosis, brain tumors or strokes to develop Clinical Depression at some point during the course of their illness.

The risk also increases for cancer sufferers. In some cases, like that of pancreatic cancer, Clinical Depression happens before other signs of the illness. Table 2.2 lists some of the medical illnesses that increase risk for depression.

Table 2.2 Some medical illnesses that can increase the risk for depression

Parkinson's disease

Multiple sclerosis

Dementia

Head injury

Thyroid disease

Diabetes

Liver disease

Cancer

Tuberculosis

Syphilis

AIDS

Hypertension

4. Drug and/or Alcohol Abuse

". . . I was an abuser of alcohol and had used recreational drugs in the past. I felt trapped and lost all hope. It was during a weekend of binge drinking that I became so despondent that I tried to commit suicide. Luckily my wife was there to stop me. At that point, she made me tell my primary care physician with the HMO we were with what was happening to me."

Drugs and alcohol are substances that quickly and dramatically alter mood. Alcohol is widely known to be a substance that can lower and depress mood. Heavy drinkers, and those who abuse alcohol, increase their risk for developing Clinical Depression. The same is true for many other substances, including illegal substances like heroin and cocaine.

In the case of alcohol, distinguishing between social drinking and problem drinking can be difficult. There are four key questions that can help you assess whether drinking is a problem for you. They are shown in Table 2.3.

Table 2.3 Is alcohol a special problem for me? A "yes" answer to any one of these questions may indicate that you have a drinking problem.

In the last month, was there a single day in which you had five or more drinks of beer, wine, or liquor?	YES NO
Did you ever think that you were an excessive drinker?	YES NO
Has there ever been a period of two weeks when you were drinking seven or more alcoholic drinks (beer, wine, or other alcoholic beverage) a day?	YES NO
Have you ever drunk as much as a fifth of liquor in one day? (That would be about twenty drinks or three bottles of wine or as much as three six-packs of beer in one day.)	YES, more than once YES, but only once NO

Kathryn Rost, M. Audrey Burnam, G. Richard Smith. Development of Screeners for Depressive Disorders and Substance Disorder History. *Medical Care* Vol.31, Number 3, pp. 189–200.

Answering "yes" to any one of these questions signals a potential problem with alcohol. Answering "yes" to more than two questions increases the likelihood of a serious drinking problem. If you answer "yes" to any question, you should talk to your doctor about your drinking habits.

Any addictive substance can alter mood and bring about depressive symptoms. Such substances include amphetamines like Dexedrine and Methedrine, inhalants like airplane glue, cocaine, heroin, psychedelic drugs like LSD, opioids like morphine and heroin, and phencyclidine (PCP).

5. Prescription Medications

Depression is a potential side effect of many kinds of prescription medications. Some people are more sensitive to this effect than others. Usually, only a small number of people on any given medication will develop Clinical Depression.

Researchers theorize that, in some individuals, these medications alter brain chemicals. Fortunately, the effects are reversible. The symptoms go away when the doctor discontinues the medication.

Table 2.4 lists some of the types of medicines that have depression as a potential side effect. Again, not every person who takes one of these drugs will develop Clinical Depression as a side effect. Still, if you are taking a medication from any of these groups, this is information you should have.

Table 2.4 Medications linked to clinical depression

Cancer drugs

Pain medications

Heart medications

Blood pressure medications

Hormones, including birth control pills

Nerve and brain disease medications

Some antibiotics

6. Exposure to Physical and/or Sexual Violence

"My marriage was a disaster. . . There was domestic violence before that was recognized, deception, infidelity, verbal and psychological abuse. I did not realize all of this was causing me to be depressed."

Victims of physical or sexual abuse, and those living in circumstances where violence is a constant threat, have a higher-than-average risk of developing depression. Victims of rape and other assault also carry a high risk.

Living in unsafe situations, either in the home or in the community, also increases the chance that you will develop serious symptoms. Severe physical and emotional trauma often lead to Clinical Depression.

7. Poverty

"Living by myself; taking care of my home and yard, and being a senior citizen on a small monthly income have been factors in my having down periods."

Living in poverty is another condition that carries a high risk for developing Clinical Depression. The everyday struggle to make ends meet can take a terrible toll. Those who don't have enough money, who have to make a great effort to provide food, clothing, and shelter for themselves and their families are much more likely to become discouraged, disheartened, and develop depression. For the poor who are unemployed, the situation is especially difficult, because they may not have the means to get help. It's a myth that the depressed don't get depressed.

8. Past History of Clinical Depression

"At my present age of 38. . . I will need to go back to my teen years, when I started dealing with depression. My first remembrance with depression started at the age of 13. . . "

Experiencing one episode of Clinical Depression, unfortunately, increases your chance of having another bout of this illness sometime during your lifetime. About half of those diagnosed with Clinical Depression go on to have a second episode. About 70% of those with a history of two episodes go on to have a third.[6] The risk of future depression appears to increase with each additional episode. The reasons for this are not clear.

A very small number go on to have a series of depressive episodes. In these cases, the illness appears to happen in cycles, with periods of depression occurring between phases of normal mood. Symptom-free phases can last for years.

It is especially important for people who experience several bouts of depression to learn the early warning signs of Depression so that they can get immediate treatment. Some may need to stay on treatment even when they're feeling well.

9. Hormonal Change

"I have been depressed about four times in my 61 years on earth. The first was right after the birth of my first child. Hormonal changes and lack of sleep, as well as a demanding baby, seemed to be some of the causes."

Hormones are chemical substances that circulate throughout the body helping your cells to function normally. They regulate the body's metabolism and can also affect thought, feelings, and behaviors. Internal organs called *glands* produce them.

Clinicians long ago discovered that people with glandular diseases often have dramatic changes in their mood. Depressive symptoms occur commonly in diseases of the thyroid, the adrenals, and are also seen in diabetes, a disease of the pancreas.

A woman's ovaries produce the female hormones estrogen and progesterone. It is normal for the levels of both of these hormones to change during a woman's monthly menstrual cycle. They also shift dramatically during and immediately after a woman gives birth.

Some women experience uncomfortable feelings during different phases of their menstrual cycle. They notice that they get particularly "edgy" a few days before starting their menstrual period. They become unusually irritable, tearful, and are more easily upset.

These symptoms usually last three or four days, then go away as soon as a woman starts menstruating. A small number of women have symptoms so severe that they have trouble dealing with people at home and at work. They may have a rare disorder called Pre-Menstrual Syndrome (PMS). An important difference between PMS and Clinical Depression is that women with PMS basically feel normal and in control most other days of their monthly cycle. Their symptoms are temporary.

Moodiness, irritability, and other emotional changes can also happen to women going through menopause. Menopause, which is sometimes called the "change of life," is that time in early to late middle age when women stop menstruating and can no longer become pregnant. Besides moodiness, though, menopausal women usually have other complaints, like hot flashes, which help identify this normal stage of life.

When menopausal symptoms become intolerable, or when symptoms seriously interfere with a woman's day-to-day life, clinicians administer female hormones to help decrease the discomfort.

The first few weeks after giving birth are a time when female hormone levels rapidly shift. Many new mothers complain of feeling down or a little blue immediately after giving birth. This is commonly called "the baby blues." However, there is a very serious form of Clinical Depression, called *Postpartum Depression*, which begins days to weeks after a woman gives birth. Women who have Postpartum Depression experience a very severe form of depression that can include symptoms of strange, even bizarre, ideas and suspicious thoughts about others, especially their children. Someone with this form of depressive illness needs immediate help. We discuss Postpartum Depression in the section describing different types of Clinical Depression.

10. Social Isolation

People who are socially isolated and those who feel that they have little or no emotional support in their lives are more vulnerable to becoming clinically depressed. Those who live alone may be more likely to experience loneliness; however, individuals living with others can also feel forlorn and extremely lonely.

DEPRESSION THAT COMES "OUT OF THE BLUE"

"You can be so successful, and one day depression really gets the better of you and you can't function without that outside help. A person's mind can be so unpredictable; so many things can influence it. I work every day to keep going, taking one day at a time."

Clinical Depression can happen without any risk factors. People who don't experience terrible events or bad circumstances can also become seriously depressed. Their lives may be going well when, without warning, their mood begins a downward plunge. The depression seems to come from nowhere, without warning. There is no obvious explanation for their negative feelings and behaviors. This can be especially confusing for sufferers and their loved ones.

Potential Protective Factors

"I think at times in your life [there are]certain situations or circumstances [that] can help you through your depression, [and they] can also add to it. The truth is it is always there that [it is the] chemical imbalance in the brain that threatens your life every day, even if [you're] not aware of it."

Just as we don't know exactly what causes depression, we don't know exactly how to prevent it. We do know that there are peo-

29

ple with significant risk factors who do not become depressed. It's possible that there are protective factors. That's an area for future research.

TYPES OF CLINICAL DEPRESSION

What we know about depression comes primarily from clinicians. Their clinical knowledge came from talking with and observing their patients. Experts, using this information, noted that groups of patient varied in terms of the types of symptoms they experienced and the course of the illness. Our current diagnostic categories come from these direct observations.

It is clear now that just as there are several kinds of arthritis, there are several types of Clinical Depression. *Clinical Depression* is the general term that describes a broad-spectrum of clinical ailments. All share similar clusters of symptoms, but they differ in quantity, quality, and duration of symptoms. The specific diagnosis depends on the particular kinds of symptoms, the number of symptoms, how long symptoms last, and the degrees to which symptoms interfere with the ability to perform routine daily activities.

The following section lists the most common diagnoses in Clinical Depression and describes the most important or signature features of each disorder. Our terminology follows that of *The Diagnostic and Statistical Manual of Mental Disorders* (DSM-IV), a text used by trained medical and mental-health professionals to diagnose emotional disorders.

Even though Clinical Depression is not a recent illness, much of the information that we have about it is new. Because of this, diagnostic procedures and treatment are in an ongoing process of development. When clinicians learn more about the biology of depression, they may find it more helpful to differentiate depressive disorders by the ways particular brain chemicals or medications work. In the future, with new and better information, clinicians will probably revise current categories or even devise an entirely different system of classification.

A. *Major Depressive Disorder*

One of the most common forms of Clinical Depression is a disease known as *Major Depressive Disorder*. Somewhere between 10 to 25 out of every 100 women (10 to 25%) and 5 to 12 out of every 100 men (5 to 12%) experience this disorder at some point in their lives. The word "major" gives an indication of the level of impairment experienced by those with this form of mood dysfunction. Major depression is one of the most severe and disabling forms of depression. Another name for this illness is *Unipolar Depression*, a term used to distinguish it from *Bipolar Disorder*, another form of mood disorder.

The two primary conditions needed to make this diagnosis are: (1) the depressive symptoms must represent a definite change from how a person usually feels in everyday life, and (2) a person must experience symptoms *all day, almost every day*, throughout the same two-week period. Although a person may suffer with all of the symptoms described, for the diagnosis of Major Depressive Disorder, they need only have five.

The following section describes the criteria used to diagnose Major Depressive Disorder and divides them into "Feelings," "Thoughts," and "Behaviors." Table 2.5 lists these same symptoms according to the *Psychiatric Diagnostic and Statistical Manual*. People with Major Depressive Disorder must have at least five of the following symptoms, with depressed mood or decreased interest (or pleasure) in enjoyable activities being one of them.

Table 2.5 DSM-IV Diagnostic Criteria for Major Depression[6]

Criteria for Major Depressive Episode

A. Five (or more) of the following symptoms have been present during the same 2-week period and represent a change from previous functioning; at least one of the symptoms is either (1) depressed mood or (2) loss of interest or pleasure.

Note: Do not include symptoms that are clearly due to a general medical condition, or mood-incongruent delusions or hallucinations.

   (1) *depressed mood most of the day, nearly every day, as indicated by either subjective report (e.g., feels sad or empty) or observation made by others (e.g., appears tearful).* **Note**: *In children and adolescents, can be irritable mood.*

   (2) *markedly diminished interest or pleasure in all, or almost all, activities most of the day, nearly every day (as indicated by either subjective account or observation made by others).*

   (3) *significant weight loss when not dieting or weight gain (e.g., a change of more than 5% of body weight in a month), or decrease or increase in appetite nearly every day.* **Note**: *In children, consider failure to make expected weight gains.*

   (4) *insomnia or hypersomnia nearly ever day.*

   (5) *psychomotor agitation or retardation nearly every day (observable by others, not merely subjective feelings of restlessness or being slowed down).*

   (6) *fatigue or loss of energy nearly every day.*

   (7) *feelings of worthlessness or excessive or inappropriate guilt (which may be delusional) nearly every day (not merely self-reproach or guilt about being sick).*

   (8) *diminished ability to think or concentrate, or indecisiveness, nearly every day (either by subjective account or as observed by others).*

   (9) *recurrent thoughts of death (not just fear of dying), recurrent suicidal ideation without a specific plan, or a suicide attempt or a specific plan for committing suicide.*

B. The symptoms do meet criteria for a Mixed Episode.

C. The symptoms cause clinically significant distress or impairment in social, occupational, or other important areas of functioning.

D. The symptoms are not due to the direct physiological effects of the substance (e.g., a drug of abuse, a medication) or a general medical condition (e.g., hypothyroidism).

E. The symptoms are not better accounted for by Bereavement, i.e., after the loss of a loved one, the symptoms persist for longer than 2 months or are characterized by marked functional impairment, morbid preoccupation with worthlessness, suicidal ideation, psychotic symptoms, or psychomotor retardation.

Reprinted with permission from the *Diagnostic and Statistical Manual of Mental Disorders*, Fourth Edition, Text Revision. Copyright 2000 American Psychiatric Association.

Feelings

1. Feeling sad, downhearted, hopeless or blue most of the day, just about every day.

2. Losing interest in nearly all activities, especially hobbies or other things that used to give pleasure and happiness.

3. Feeling tired or fatigued almost all of the time, even when getting enough rest.

4. Feeling worthless or very guilty about things that previously didn't bother you. Some may feel more nervous and anxious than usual.

Thoughts

5. Pessimistic thoughts, thinking a lot about death, including ideas about suicide.

6. Slowed thinking with problems concentrating, making simple decisions, or paying attention while doing things like reading or watching television.

Behaviors

7. a) Eating much less than usual because of poor appetite, losing a significant amount of weight without intentional dieting, *or*
   b) Eating much more than usual and gaining a great deal of weight in a short period of time.

8. a) Moving much more slowly while doing things like walking or getting dressed *or*
   b) Restlessness and agitation with trouble sitting still.

9. Trouble with sleep, including either:
   a) Problems falling asleep, waking earlier than usual, waking throughout the night *or*
   b) Sleeping much more than usual.

As you can see from the above list, many sufferers of Major Depressive Disorder have a feeling of relentless sadness, while, for others, the most troubling symptom is that of not being able to experience joy or pleasure. Almost everyone with depression loses his or her sense of energy and vitality. At their lowest point, some decide that life is not worth living. Because of this, Major Depressive Disorder carries a very high risk for suicide. Fifteen out of every 100 sufferers (15%) eventually kill themselves.

There are three forms or "sub-types" of Major Depressive Disorder. Clinicians primarily base these categories on the number of symptoms experienced and the degree to which symptoms interfere with daily activities. These sub-types are Mild Major Depressive Disorder, Moderate Major Depressive Disorder, and Severe Major Depressive Disorder without or with psychotic features.

Mild Major Depressive Disorder

People with Mild Major Depressive Disorder have five or six of the nine listed symptoms and are able to make it through the day without significant impairment. They feel much worse than usual and, although they are still able to manage household activities and work, they must put forth a tremendous amount of effort to do so.

Moderate Major Depressive Disorder

People with Moderate Major Depressive Disorder usually have more than five of the nine listed symptoms. The key characteristic of this category of Major Depressive Disorder is that tremendous amounts of effort no longer work. Trying harder doesn't help sufferers keep up with things at work and at home.

They usually experience a lot of difficulty taking on and completing assignments at work. Some have trouble getting out of bed and frequently call in sick. Taking care of their children or elderly family members is often beyond them. Taking on new tasks becomes impossible as life slowly unravels.

Severe-Major Depressive Disorder without and with Psychotic Features

People with Severe Major Depressive Disorder can no longer work or manage things at home. Some stop taking care of themselves and neglect things like washing up or getting dressed. Their symptoms are so severe that they really cannot function. Some lose their jobs or stop going to work, because they have such difficulty performing simple tasks.

In the most extreme form of this illness, sufferers begin to hallucinate or have bizarre thoughts about themselves or others. They may hear voices saying bad things about them or telling them to do things to harm themselves or others. They may feel that family members are plotting against them or are out to harm them in some way. Sometimes they feel that their body is not their own or that family members are imposters. These are all symptoms of *psychosis*, a thought disorder where sufferers lose the capacity to decide what is real and what is not.

B. *Postpartum Depression*

Most new mothers experience weepiness, fatigue, frustration, and discomfort the first few days after giving birth. Learning to cope with a wonderful but demanding new infant, while dealing with sweeping body and biological changes, is not easy.

Women, during this time, may feel mildly depressed, but these emotions don't last more than a few days. This syndrome, known as the *"Baby Blues,"* can affect as many as eight out of every 10 (80%) new mothers. This is *not* a serious condition. Women get better quickly, usually within two weeks.

Postpartum Depression is not the "baby blues." It is a **serious** form of Clinical Depression. It affects between one and two out of every 10 (10 to 20%) new mothers and begins within the first four weeks of giving birth.

The symptoms seen in Postpartum Depression are identical to those seen in Major Depressive Disorder and can be just as severe. Symptoms usually start during the first month after giving birth. These new mothers become profoundly depressed and complain of not feeling like their usual selves. Unlike with "the blues," these feelings get progressively worse instead of getting better and some women become suicidal.

At the most severe stage of Postpartum Depression, women can begin to have bizarre, frightening thoughts about their babies. Some have thoughts of hurting or even killing their children. They lose the ability to distinguish what is real from what is unreal. Some hallucinate. The name of this tragic syndrome is Postpartum Psychosis. It occurs in one to two out of every 1,000 (0.2%) new mothers.

C. Dysthymic Disorder

"I believe my depression was always a part of my life, a chemical imbalance from childhood and through my teens. I was one of the lucky teenagers who made it through even though it wasn't recognized."

Dysthymic Disorder is a chronic form of Clinical Depression and affects about 6% (six out of every 100) of the general population. People with Dysthymic Disorder typically have fewer symptoms than those with Major Depressive Disorder. They suffer with symptoms for longer periods than is seen with other forms of depression, however. Dysthymic Disorder can last for years.

As with Major Depressive Disorder, in Dysthymic Disorder symptoms last for most of the day, almost every day. For a diagnosis of Dysthymic Disorder, symptoms must be present for at least *two years*. During this two-year period, some sufferers have weeks when they feel much better; however, this never lasts longer than one or two months.

Because symptoms last longer, people with Dysthymic Disorder find that it saps their energy. Even though they usually have fewer symptoms that those with Major Depression, research studies show that their functioning and quality of life is quite low.

The next section lists the criteria for a Diagnosis of Dysthymic Disorder. Table 2.6 lists them according to the DSM-IV. Symptoms are disturbing enough to interfere with day-to-day functioning. For this diagnosis, in addition to feeling depressed, people must have at least two of the following symptoms:

Feelings

1. Feeling hopeless

2. Feeling worthless or inferior to others. Feeling more worried and anxious.

Thoughts

3. Trouble concentrating, paying attention, or making decisions.

Behaviors

4. Significant change in your eating pattern with decreased or increased appetite.

5. Sleeping less or sleeping more than usual.

6. Experiencing low energy with increased tiredness and fatigue.

Table 2.6 DSM IV Diagnostic Criteria for Dysthymic Disorder

Diagnostic Criteria for 300.4 Dysthymic Disorder

A. Depressed mood for the most of the day, for more days than not, as indicated either by subjective account or observation by others, for at least 2 years. Note: In children and adolescents, mood can be irritable and duration must be at least 1 year.

B. Presence, while depressed, of two (or more) of the following:

1. *poor appetite or overeating*
2. *insomnia or hypersomnia*
3. *low energy or fatigue*
4. *low self-esteem*
5. *poor concentration or difficulty making decisions*
6. *feelings of hopelessness*

C. During the 2-year period (1 year for children or adolescents) of the disturbance, the person has never been without the symptoms in Criteria A and B for more than 2 months at a time.

D. No Major Depressive Episode has been present during the first 2 years of the Disturbance (1 year for children and adolescents); i.e., the disturbance is not better accounted for by chronic Major Depressive Disorder, or Major Depressive Disorder, In Partial Remission.

Note: There may have been a previous Major Depressive Episode provided there was a full remission (no significant signs or symptoms for 2 months) before development of the Dysthymic Disorder. In addition, after the initial 2 years (1 year in children or adolescents) of Dysthymic Disorder, there may be superimposed episodes of Major Depressive Disorder, in which case both diagnoses may be given when the criteria are met for a Major Depressive Episode.

E. There has never been a Manic Episode, a Mixed Episode, or a Hypomanic Episode, and criteria have never been met for Cyclothymic Disorder.

F. The disturbance does not occur exclusively during the course of a chronic Psychotic Disorder, as Schizophrenia or Delusional Disorder.

G. The symptoms are not due to the direct physiological effects of a substance (e.g., a drug of abuse, a medication) or general medical condition (e.g., hypothyroidism).

H. The symptoms cause clinically significant distress or impairment in social, occupational, or other important areas of functioning.

Specify if:

Early onset: if onset is before age 21 years

Late onset: if onset is age 21 years or older

Specify (for most recent 2 years of Dysthymic Disorder):

With Atypical Features

Reprinted with permission from the *Diagnostic and Statistical Manual of Mental Disorders*, Fourth Edition, Text Revision. Copyright 2000 American Psychiatric Association.

It is possible to have Major Depressive Disorder and Dysthymic Disorder at the same time. This happens when someone with Dysthymic Disorder develops an acute episode of Major Depression. The number of symptoms increases and they have more trouble performing their usual activities. When people with Dysthymic Disorder develop symptoms that match those seen in Major Depressive Disorder, they have what is referred to as "Double Depression." Clinicians use this term when a person has both of these disorders.

D. Minor Depression

Minor Depressive Disorder is a relatively new category of Clinical Depression. The specific criteria are still in the process of development. Recent research studies revealed it to be a separate form of Clinical Depression. Minor Depression has its own distinct characteristics.

Minor Depressive Disorder is less severe than Major Depressive Disorder and appears to cause much less distress and difficulty in keeping up with average daily activities. People with Minor Depressive Disorder may have some of the same symptoms as those with Major Depressive Disorder; but they have fewer symptoms. The term "minor" does not reflect the seriousness of this illness. It refers to the fact that sufferers typically have fewer symptoms than with other forms of depression. Between two and four symptoms are enough to meet criteria for this diagnosis. As with other forms of Clinical Depression, symptoms must be present nearly all day, almost every day, for a period of at least two weeks. There is evidence that people with Minor Depression are at higher risk for developing either Major Depressive or Dysthymic Disorder.

E. Other Disorders with Depressive Symptoms and/or Clinical Depression

There are some groups of people who experience depressive symptoms during the course of another illness or disorder. At times, their symptoms may be severe or significant enough to justify adding Clinical Depression to their list of ailments.

Depression Due to General Medical Condition

People with general medical illness, especially serious general medical illness (diabetes, hypertension, stroke, heart disease, cancer, HIV-AIDS, Parkinson's disease, and others), frequently experience some of the same symptoms seen in Clinical Depression. Approximately one out of every four (20 to 25%) people experiences an episode of Clinical Depression while medically ill.

In general, this form of depression is diagnosed when the symptoms of depression can be directly connected to the course of the general medical illness. For example, if the depressive symptoms start with the onset of the medical illness, or if the depressive symptoms begin when the illness gets worse and get better when the medical illness improves, chances are good that Clinical Depression is a secondary consequence of having a medical disease.

Suicidal thoughts are a particular concern for those with chronic severe pain or diseases that have no known cure. They carry a higher than average risk of making a suicidal attempt.

Bipolar Disorder (also known as Manic Depressive Disorder)

Besides Dysthymic Disorder, there are other mood syndromes known to have a chronic or recurring course. Bipolar Disorder is one of them. Manic Depression is another name for Bipolar Disorder.

People with this disorder experience both extremes of mood. They can have severe depression and at other times have symptoms described as mania. A person experiencing mania behaves and thinks in dramatically different ways from her usual way of thinking and behaving. Mania includes the following disquieting symptoms:

Feelings

1. Feeling that you are better or smarter than everyone else, including feeling that you have special insights or powers that others don't have.

2. Feeling much more energetic than usual, in fact, so energetic than you can't sit still.

3. Becoming irritable and easily angered by others, sometimes becoming violent.

Thoughts

4. Thinking much faster than usual, as if thoughts are racing at an incredible speed. This may also include having lots of new ideas, but not being able to think them through clearly.

Behaviors

5. Talking much more than usual and not being able to keep silent when necessary.

6. Sleeping a lot less, but feeling energized instead of tired.

7. Engaging in risky activities, such as spending lots of money even when money is tight, or having more sexual encounters or many more sexual partners than usual and not caring about the danger of contracting a sexually transmitted disease.

People with Bipolar Disorder also have episodes that are identical to Major Depression. The word "bipolar" means that they experience two radically different types of mood. At times they are very "up" and at other times very "down." Between episodes, they usually have a normal mood.

Earlier, in the section on Major Depressive Disorder, the term *Unipolar Depression* was used. The term for multiple episodes of Major Depression is Unipolar Depression. People with Unipolar Depression only experience the "down" pole of mood. As with Bipolar Disorder, there may be years of normal, healthy functioning between depressive episodes. The phrase "Major Depressive Disorder" describes a current single episode.

Bipolar illness can be a disabling illness, and is perhaps more disabling on average than the other types of mood disorders discussed in this chapter. In the Partners in Care study, we found that patients with symptoms suggestive of bipolar illness had worse functioning and quality of life than the other patients with depression.

Posttraumatic Stress Disorder

Posttraumatic Stress Disorder is a disease that develops in some people after they personally experienced (or witnessed) either a life-threatening event or an incident that threatened serious bodily injury. These events include things like: violent assault, as is the case with rape or physical attack (with or without a weapon); war or military combat; natural disasters, such as earthquakes, hurricane, floods, volcanic eruptions; or serious accidents such as can happen with car and airplane crashes. The terrorist attacks of September 11, 2001, were such events. The attacks killed thousands and injured many more.

People with this disorder have trouble with recurrent thoughts and nightmares about the event. While awake, they can have flashbacks that make them "relive" the trauma. Besides experiencing severe distress and unhappiness, they have trouble sleeping; concentrating, and can have angry or violent outbursts.

As with Clinical Depression, their symptoms often interfere with their ability to have a normal life. They feel depressed from time to time, but they don't usually experience the same number of symptoms or the severity of symptoms experienced by those with Clinical Depression. Like Double Depression, it is possible to have both Posttraumatic Stress Disorder and Clinical Depression.

Adjustment Disorders

There is a group of clinical disorders called "Adjustment Disorders" that can be seen as milder forms of posttraumatic stress. People with Adjustment Disorders experience stressful or unhappy events, but they are not life-threatening and do not involve serious physical injury. Events can be serious setbacks such as an abrupt change in finances, divorce, losing a loved one through forced separation or death, being fired or laid off, and adjusting to stressful new circumstances. There may be multiple events or more than one thing that causes distress.

People with Adjustment Disorder have far fewer depressive symptoms than those seen in other forms of Clinical Depression and they are able to carry on their normal lives without much effort. Depressed feelings typically start within three months of the incident and usually get better or resolve by six months.

If a person has the same number of symptoms listed for Major Depressive Disorder, Minor Depressive Disorder, and Dysthymic Disorder, they do not have a simple Adjustment Disorder. If they have many symptoms and have trouble when they try to manage things, they probably have a more serious form of Clinical Depression.

Seasonal Pattern Depression

"I suffer with Seasonal Affective Disorder. When daylight savings time is over, I want to hibernate."

Some people with Clinical Depression only experience symptoms at particular times of the year. Their depression shows a seasonal pattern. Depressive episodes typically start during the fall or winter months and resolve during the spring and summer months. This is called Seasonal Pattern Depression or Seasonal Affective Disorder.

This form of depression happens more often in climates with long hours of darkness during the fall and winter months. Seasonal Affective Disorder is more common in the far northern regions of the globe—places like Scandinavia, Alaska and Iceland.

This chapter presented information about the risk factors for Clinical Depression. It also talked at some length about the different types of clinical depression. Learning about different forms of depression is important, because clinical treatment varies by the severity and type of symptoms. For the most part, different disorders require different types of treatment regimens. The next few chapters will describe all of this in detail.

Clinical Depression can be a difficult illness, but good treatments do exist. The next section introduces you to two people who were kind enough to share their stories.

LETTERS FROM THE HEART: STORIES OF DEPRESSION

For people with depression, it's important to know that they are not alone in how they feel. Although depression impacts people in different ways, nearly everyone with serious depression has periods of feeling utterly lost and alone. Many feel that there is no way for them to get help.

During the Partners in Care study, we received letters from many people with depression. These letters provide a glimpse into how the experience of depression affects each individual. What is similar is the pain and sense of loss.

We include some of their letters and/or quotes throughout this book. We hope that they can help sufferers and their loved ones understand that they are truly not alone.

This first letter is a translation from the original Spanish.

"To Whom it May Concern:

Thank you beforehand for the attention you have given me. I'm writing you this small letter.

"My problem, or the reason for my profound sadness, is due to the fact that I was a woman excited about the birth of her first child who never thought that what she thought would complete her happiness, the birth of her child, would be completely different. Her little girl was born with cerebral palsy.

"It has been two years, and I can assure you that they have been the saddest and toughest ones I've lived. As you know, there are more difficult times ahead, and only God knows what our destiny holds in store. It's true I am very sad, but there's a little girl who needs me and her father and we will be with her for as long as she needs us. I have to put my suffering aside for my little girl whom I love very much and I ask God to keep her forever and to give me the strength to care for my little angel.

"I tell you these things to let you know that personally I feel like no one, no one could help me find solace and resignation. I can't. I can leave things as they are, live life as it presents itself, but God knows that day after day my mother's grief is always present, even though there are days when I'm even more depressed. And I do have very difficult days, especially when someone says to me, "Have a nice day." To me, these words are foreign and to be honest, I feel bitter towards life itself. It's been two years where I've known no happiness. And God knows how I long to be happy. But with my little girl, who can't even look at me: How? I thank you for your attention, and I am at your service."

This heartfelt letter emphasizes the point that Clinical Depression can start after a serious life event. This woman's words reveal her struggle with sadness and grief. Her letter also shows her deep love for her daughter. She has tremendous courage and strength, but her situation is very difficult, and she is depressed.

The next letter demonstrates that the sheer weight of mounting problems can finally result in Clinical Depression.

"To Whom it May Concern:

You have my apologies. My diabetes has become a major problem with the muscular neuropathy getting so painful that on some days I can hardly walk. I have gotten a treadmill, but my performance on it has gotten poorer rather than better. I lost my best client, something I had anticipated, but didn't wish to face, so my income has dropped drastically and I don't know how to go about recovering. Everything I have touched in the stock market has plunged, while the market is booming all around me. . .

"In the last couple of months, my grandfather had a pancreatitis attack, recovered, and then had to be placed in a nursing home. My grandmother has had a double bypass and a valve replacement in her heart. She is recovering, but not very rapidly. I have been very close to my grandparents. . . My father had quadruple bypass surgery, and it looked like we might lose him for a while, but he has now recovered. The trouble is, it almost seems as if he doesn't care whether he lives or dies, and does nothing that might prolong his life. I've tried to convince myself that it's his problem, not mine, but that still nags at the back of my mind. A close friend of the family died last month, and within a few days another died. . .

"My wife and I sleep in separate bedrooms. We have had no physical relations for over ten years. My son moved back into the house and stirred the pot by telling her she would not be happy living here, and should move out. . . We discussed it and she said she was comfortable living with me, so she didn't want to leave. Needless to say, things are a bit strained between us.

"My oldest son suddenly appeared at the house (as distinguished from a home) with a packed suitcase and announced he was moving in until he and his wife got a few things straightened out. He stayed for three or four days and disappeared as suddenly as he appeared.

"I crave some sort of affection. I raised my children with affection, love, and touching, and it seems to have [affected] their relationships positively, but they are gone. The only affection and love I receive is from a cat who just wants to be fed and let in and out of the house.

"Soap Opera City? Truth is stranger than fantasy. . . .

"Am I depressed? By my definition, yes. Do I feel alone with it? No. I'm sure others have it worse. Do I feel unique about my problems? Some of them. Do I want to take drugs or tell others about them [in treatment]? No. This is as close as it is going to come [by writing this letter]. Do I feel that anyone else can help me or relieve me of some of the burdens? No. Why?

"My physical problems are either brought on by my own feelings or by chemical imbalances. I work on the feelings, the doctor works on the chemical imbalances. My depression is my own. Sharing it doesn't solve it. Drugs only serve to mask it. The responsibility is mine and mine alone. . .

"No, I don't want out of my shell, for several reasons, the most important being that every time I have ever lowered my barriers I have been betrayed, hurt, or humiliated to the core. Human beings don't want to understand; they want the knowledge to destroy at their leisure. . . .

"The replies [in this letter] might astound you, or you might find that they fit right in with other profiles."

A different person could have written each paragraph of the above letter. There are so many events that lead to depression, but all of these problems were experienced by the same man! Readers can sense his despair, self-blame, and reluctance to believe that treatment can help. The depression seems so much a part of his overwhelming life problems that it's hard for him to feel that treatment truly can relieve depressive symptoms even though his life problems remain.

The good news is that by getting treatment known to be effective for depression, wide ranges of people with depression improve—even people like those who have written these moving letters.

In the next two chapters, we explain what treatments for depression are effective and how to go about getting these treatments.

CHAPTER 3

I THINK I'M CLINICALLY DEPRESSED. WHAT ARE MY OPTIONS?

"Once I recognized the problem and surmounted the traditional societal attitudes toward depression, I received—and continue to receive—superb care."

If you recognize yourself or a family member in the sections describing depressive symptoms, there's a good possibility that you (or they) have some form of Clinical Depression. Remember, depression is a common disorder. In any given year, it affects one out of every 10 men (10%) and two out of every 10 women (20%). The good news is that there is hope. Just like asthma or hypertension, Clinical Depression is a treatable illness. There are many excellent treatments available to alleviate the emotional pain and distress.

The last decades of the twentieth century witnessed an explosion of information about the nature and course of depressive illness. Public awareness grew as research discovered the widespread nature of the disorder. Clinical trials and national surveys confirmed that depression happens to people of all ages, races, religions, creeds, and colors.

Knowledge about depression treatments expanded as clinicians found better ways to detect and diagnose mood disorders. During this same period, scientists discovered several new classes of medication. Psychotherapists developed innovative therapies for counseling the depressed.

The Partners in Care study was one of the research trials that contributed important information about ways to improve care for the depressed. The study included adults of all ages and persons of many racial and ethnic backgrounds, including Latinos and African Americans. The study found that all groups responded to improved care.

Although a small number of people recover from depression on their own, this is very rare. Many suffer for months before starting to feel better. Depression treatment offers the hope for significant improvement. The time it takes to get well is relatively brief when compared to the time spent in misery without care.

There are many treatments and many different ways to organize them. People with depression have more options now than at any other period of history. This chapter describes current treatments and discusses their use in clinical practice.

TREATMENT OF DEPRESSION

Depression treatment falls into three basic categories—psychotherapy, pharmacotherapy, and therapeutic procedures. Psychotherapy refers to treatments that involve talking to a trained mental health specialist. Pharmacotherapy refers to management of the disorder with medications. Therapeutic procedures involve the use of medical technology and specialized equipment.

1. Psychotherapy[1]

"Slowly, with the help of the counselor, I began to crawl my way back to the living."

It may be difficult to imagine how talking can relieve symptoms or significantly impact a medical disorder. The fact is, psychotherapy is not the same as talking to a friend or neighbor.

Movies and television programs sometimes give a distorted, even unrealistic, view of what happens in psychotherapy. A psychotherapist is a trained, licensed professional who works with clients to identify problem areas and develop techniques to relieve the emotional burdens associated with Clinical Depression. Psychotherapy is guided conversation with a specific purpose.

One way to explain psychotherapy is to describe it as a specialized form of counseling. It may be best to compare the work of psychotherapists to that of coaches for professional athletes.

The best coaches use their knowledge, skills, and training to help athletes identify personal problems that keep them from functioning at their best. They then work together to design a program that can help the athletes improve their performance. Psychotherapists work in a similar way and have similar goals. They want their clients to feel better and function at their best level. They want them to enjoy life. They do this by helping them understand their feelings, thoughts, and behaviors. Together, they develop strategies to cope with symptoms and personal problems.

The term *psychotherapy* covers a broad range of theories, approaches, and techniques. There are many different types of psychotherapy. As with other clinical treatments, a person's individual needs and preferences determine the type of psychotherapy best suited for them.

Of the current therapies, two were developed specifically for people diagnosed with Clinical Depression: Interpersonal Therapy and Cognitive Behavioral Therapy. Therapists also use Psychodynamic Psychotherapy and Supportive Psychotherapy to treat people who are depressed. The next section describes some of the therapies used to treat depressed people.

A. Interpersonal Therapy (IPT)[2]

Interpersonal Therapy is a form of therapy designed to help identify the events, people, or circumstances that precipitate or worsen depression. The theory behind this form of therapy is that bad events and difficult relationships play a major role in triggering depressive symptoms.

Therapists who conduct Interpersonal Therapy help their clients single out those personal interactions that cause distress and produce depressed or unhappy feelings. After understanding these triggers, the therapist and client work to modify or change the person's way of interacting and responding to difficult situations.

An example of this would be the case of Mary. Mary S.* was feeling profoundly depressed. She slept poorly and felt tired all the time. She was unhappy in her marriage, because her husband liked to argue. They fought all the time and he didn't treat her well. Because she worked as a receptionist and didn't earn much money, her family kept telling her to stay in the relationship. He had a high-paying job and they saw him as "a good provider." Mary was demoralized and discouraged. She didn't know what to do. She talked the situation over with her family doctor. The doctor suggested a psychotherapy consultation. The therapist recommended Interpersonal Therapy.

In Interpersonal Therapy, the therapist helped Mary recognize the emotional consequences of living in an unhappy, physically abusive relationship. The two of them discussed her reasons for staying with this man. They explored the odds of improving the relationship and looked at the option of ending it. They also identified techniques for enlisting the support of her family. Mary, also, learned ways to keep herself safe. Her sleep improved and she started feeling better. Faced with the possibility of divorce, her husband agreed to counseling.

*Not a real person—a composite.

Mary's abusive marriage and lack of family support were two key sources of her depressed feelings. The road to getting better started with this realization.

In summary, Interpersonal Therapy helps identify the circumstances that contribute to, or increase, the symptoms of depression. This therapy helps sufferers find ways to change or modify things that make them feel worse. The primary focus is on resolving relationship problems and their emotional consequences. By improving a person's ability to manage relationships, this therapy helps smooth the transition into wellness.

Interpersonal Therapy is a short-term therapy that lasts from three to four months. Each session focuses on improving interpersonal issues. Weekly sessions last for about 50 minutes.

"My sense of desperation is gone. I do not feel so alone and helpless in combating my day-to-day problems. My anger has subsided to the point that people see me differently (because I am different!) and my relationships with people have improved dramatically."

B. Cognitive Behavioral Therapy (CBT)[3]

Cognitive Behavioral Therapy is another short-term therapy developed for those with Clinical Depression. The word *cognitive* refers to the process of thinking: in other words, how people think and what they believe.

People with Clinical Depression undergo cognitive changes. During the depression, their thoughts and beliefs about themselves, others, and the world become deeply pessimistic. Depressed people are especially hopeless about themselves.

The theory behind Cognitive Behavioral Therapy is that negative thinking is rooted in distorted beliefs. These negative thoughts contribute to depressive symptoms. The symptoms begin a vicious cycle. The thoughts activate depression, which, in turn, activates negative thinking.

Cognitive Behavioral Therapy is designed to directly combat and heal negative thinking. It stops the vicious cycle. Negative thinking includes pessimistic or overly critical opinions about oneself or others and overwhelming feelings of self-doubt. Bill's case demonstrates all of these.

Bill* had always been extremely critical of himself and others. He basically believed that the world was a terrible place. He thought it was full of people trying to take advantage of him. These feelings intensified when his wife divorced him after 35 years of marriage. He became enraged that the divorce settlement forced him to sell his house.

He continued working and moved in with an adult son until he could afford a place of his own. He quickly realized that he didn't like being around his grandchildren. He thought they were too loud and unruly.

After a few months, he started feeling hopeless and began believing that he would never get back on his feet. He felt worthless and ashamed. He avoided old friends and refused to participate in family activities.

Cognitive Behavioral Therapy with Bill focused on identifying his harmful thought patterns and revealed the impact that negative thoughts and beliefs had on his feelings and behavior. The therapist explored the links between his beliefs, his behavior, and his depression. She gently challenged some of his distorted beliefs and helped him see that not everyone was intent on taking advantage of him. She also helped Bill find ways to begin participating in enjoyable activities with friends and family.

One of his homework assignments was to visit friends and invite them to do something enjoyable. Bill chose to go to a baseball

*Not a real person—a composite.

game. They also developed a system for Bill to reward himself, a technique to reinforce the change. Bill became less skeptical as he started feeling better. He was still somewhat cynical, but gave people more of a chance.

Recent studies show that Cognitive Behavioral Therapy is particularly effective with depressed teenagers. It also seems to help some adolescents with symptoms avoid developing full-blown Major Depression.

Cognitive Behavioral Therapy can be conducted with individuals (one-on-one) or with small groups with 10 to 12 members. The therapist and client decide which is better. Sessions meet weekly, last for about 50 minutes, and continue for two to three months.

Cognitive Behavioral Therapy was the main therapy used in the Partners in Care study. This quote describes the therapy experience of one of the study participants:

> "Learning to talk back to my negative thinking and challenge my fearful outlook changed my life...I just say "no" to depression. I have developed coping strategies and I have the confidence to select and apply them to my daily life."

C. Psychodynamic Therapy
(also known as Dynamic Psychotherapy)

The word *psychodynamic* is a technical term used by mental-health specialists. It refers to the process of examining self-destructive and/or self-defeating emotions and behaviors. This therapy focuses on the inner struggles that can begin as a result of a poor match between personality and environment. Personality refers to the habitual way a person responds to others and approaches problems. In most cases, these response patterns started in childhood.

Psychodynamic Psychotherapy is based on the theory that personality characteristics can cause or perpetuate depression. In psychodynamic psychotherapy, the therapist examines a client's childhood and other life experiences. The purpose is to identify the roots of behaviors that bring unhappiness to the client or others. The theory is that insight can stimulate positive change. The overall goal is to gain insight into these characteristics so that they can modify or change the traits that interfere with the client having a full and happy life.

Let's use Sarah* as an example. Even in childhood, Sarah was painfully shy and had difficulty making friends. At 42 years old, she still had trouble meeting people and speaking up for herself. Her problems started with a lukewarm evaluation from her boss. He complained that she never spoke up in meetings and seemed overwhelmed by any new or difficult task. He also mentioned that co-workers avoided her because she never joined in conversations.

After being passed over for a much-wanted promotion, Sarah started coming in late. She called in sick several days in a row. Her boss demoted her and transferred her to a different department. Her new supervisor remarked that she seemed disinterested and always looked tired. When asked to explain herself, Sarah remained silent. The next week she got a letter telling her that she would be fired if she didn't improve. Sarah took vacation time and stayed in bed, crying, for two weeks.

The Psychodynamic therapist tried to find the reasons for Sarah's difficulties. The first step was finding insight into how Sarah's behavior began. They explored whether Sarah's current behavior began at a time when social or emotional withdrawal was the only recourse. They discovered that Sarah's behavior began at age five, after both of her parents died in an automobile accident. Her

*Not a real person—a composite.

elderly grandmother raised her. Her grandmother was uncomfortable with children and did not allow her to have friends. She grew up in a household filled with sadness and strict rules.

Over time, the therapist and Sarah came to understand her behavior. Sarah was relieved, but still needed help to learn how to change. Overcoming personality obstacles and forming fledgling friendships helped her feel better about herself and improved her symptoms.

The length of time spent in Psychodynamic Therapy is highly variable and depends on the nature of the personality problems. Dynamic therapy can last a few months to several years. The number of sessions per week also varies. Sometimes, the client and therapist meet more than once a week. As with Interpersonal Therapy and Cognitive Behavioral Therapy, each meeting lasts about 50 minutes.

Other forms of Psychodynamic Therapy include Couple's Therapy, Family Therapy, and Group Therapy. They all use the same technique, that of examining the way personality factors contribute to emotional distress. Couple's therapy explores issues causing discord in the relationship; Family Therapy examines troubling interactions among family members; and Group Therapy explores the effect of personality on the ability to form healthy social relationships.

Most community therapists practice Psychodynamic Therapy. Nonetheless, there is less scientific evidence that it works for Clinical Depression when compared to Cognitive Behavioral Therapy. One recent study of severe and chronic depression showed that some forms of Brief Psychodynamic Psychotherapy worked well. This therapy worked best for patients who also received medication.

As we stated above, there are a number of effective psychotherapies for Clinical Depression. This offers hope for people who prefer therapy to receiving medication.

"I have made a difference, because I sought help when I needed it and trusted the man I called my savior. I do believe that in order to have help during depression you have to find someone you can trust. If the first counselor doesn't help, find another. Keep going until you find the one that suits you and your needs. I went through three before I found one that I felt comfortable with."

D. Supportive Psychotherapy[4]

Supportive Therapy focuses on helping people deal with the impact of Clinical Depression on their job and family life. Because depression specifically impairs the ability to function at work and at home, many people have difficulty getting their lives back on track. Adjustment problems can continue even after depressive symptoms resolve. Supportive therapy is designed to provide additional emotional support for sufferers as they cope with making lifestyle changes that keep them feeling better. It is not known to be effective as the sole treatment for Clinical Depression.

Self-Help and Support Groups. Many self-help and social support groups are based on the principles of Supportive Psychotherapy. Organizations like the National Depressive and Manic-Depressive Association (NDMDA) offer help to depressed people and their families. There is more about this in Chapter 7, "Living with Depression."

Psychotherapy is not easy. People face the challenge of changing their feelings, thoughts, and behaviors. In the early stages, before symptoms improve, it can be painful. Although there is good evidence that Psychotherapy works, it is not appropriate for everyone. The section on treatment options gives more detail about selection criteria.

2. *Pharmacotherapy*[5]

Over the past thirty years, some of the most dramatic changes in medicine have happened in the field of medication therapy. There are now more than 20 antidepressant medications. Many of the newer medications have fewer, less troubling side effects than some of the earlier drugs. Clinicians have more choice and are better able to match the medication to the specific needs of the individual.

There are several classes of antidepressant medications. All work by affecting one or more of the neurotransmitters. As discussed in Chapter 2, neurotransmitters are chemicals thought to influence and regulate mood. Pharmacologists classify these medications according to their basic molecular structure (the way their atoms are arranged) or the way they affect neurochemicals within the brain.

Antidepressants are not like antibiotics or other drugs that give immediate relief of symptoms. They are more like thyroid and other hormone-replacement medications that take a longer time to reach their peak effect. Although individuals vary, the usual amount of time that it takes for symptoms to improve is between four and six weeks.

All medications have potential side effects. With antidepressants, many of the early side effects go away or lessen with time. Some are minor; others can be serious, even life-threatening. There is always the possibility that medications will interact with other prescription and non-prescription medications.

Antidepressant therapy must be tailored to the individual. This is especially true for children, adolescents, and the elderly. The possibility of serious side effects might seem frightening or overwhelming. Your doctor or pharmacist can help you understand the risks and help you make a good choice.

Medication treatment is an issue that must be discussed with your doctor. Each person has different requirements and circumstances. Individual needs guide the selection of medication. For this reason, we give general information about the different types of antidepressants, but *do not* give information about specific doses or guidelines on how to take them.

A. Cyclic Antidepressants

Atoms are the building blocks of all chemicals, and their arrangement determines how chemicals behave. The word "cyclic" refers to the fact that these medications have at least one ring of atoms in their chemical structure. Cyclic antidepressants block the breakdown of norepinephrine and serotonin, thereby increasing the levels of both neurotransmitters.

1. Tricyclic Antidepressants (TCAs). The name of this category of medications refers to their chemical structure. The word "tricyclic" means "three rings." Chemists looking at these compounds found that these antidepressants have the same set of atoms arranged in a ring formation in the center of their molecular structure.

Tricyclic antidepressants were among the first medications found to successfully treat Clinical Depression. They are still considered to be highly effective treatments and are often the standard used to evaluate new drugs. In clinical trials using tricyclic antidepressants, about 70 to 80% of people with Major Depressive Disorder recover fully or partially from their depression.

Nevertheless, these medications have several side effects that limit their use in some groups of patients. The elderly and people with irregular heartbeats usually cannot take these drugs.

Potential side effects and dosing schedules should be discussed with your prescribing doctor. Table 3.1 lists tricyclic medications by their generic and trade(mark) names.

Table 3.1 Tricyclic antidepressants

Generic Name	Brand Name
Amitriptyline	Elavil, Endep
Clomipramine	Anafranil
Desipramine	Norpramin, Pertofrane

Table 3.1 Tricyclic antidepressants (Cont.)

Generic Name	Brand Name
Doxepin	Adapin, Sinequan
Imipramine	Tofranil
Nortriptyline	Aventyl, Pamelor
Protriptyline	Vivactil
Trimipramine	Surmontil
Amoxapine	Asendin

2. Other Cyclic Antidepressants. Like tricyclic antidepressants, these medications also have a ring structure.However the number of rings, and kinds of atoms within the rings, differ for each of these medications. Another name for this group is "heterocyclic"* antidepressants. Their clinical effectiveness and side effects are similar to tricyclic antidepressants. Table 3.2 lists them.

Table 3.2 Heterocyclics

Generic Name	Brand Name
Maprotiline	Ludiomil
Trazodone	Desyrel

B. Selective Serotonin Reuptake Inhibitors (SSRIs)

This group of medications varies by molecular structure, but has similar selective effects on the neurotransmitter serotonin. SSRIs inhibit the breakdown of serotonin. Scientists theorize that these antidepressants elevate mood by increasing the amount of serotonin available to the brain.

Unlike earlier antidepressants, these medications can be taken once a day, most often in the morning. This can be a big advantage

* *Hetero* is derived from the Greek word meaning *different*.

to people who either tend to forget doses or do not want to take their medication at work or during other activities.

As with other antidepressant medications, SSRIs have side effects that are usually minor and go away over time. Some people experience decreased interest in sex, problems with sexual performance, and decreased enjoyment, however. These side effects don't usually go away. There are strategies to help relieve these side effects. Your doctor is the best person to help you with any physical symptoms and side effects related to medication.

Table 3.3 lists the SSRIs by generic and trade names.

Table 3.3 SSRIs

Generic Name	Brand Name
Citalopram	Celexa
Paroxetine	Paxil
Fluoxetine	Prozac
Sertraline	Zoloft
Fluvoxamine	Luvox

C. Monoamine Oxidase Inhibitors (MAOIs[6])

Monoamine oxidase is a chemical within the body, an enzyme* that breaks down two important neurotransmitters, epinephrine and serotonin. Scientists believe that MAOI medications increase the levels of both neurotransmitters by preventing this breakdown.

MAOIs are among the oldest medications used to treat Clinical Depression. Their use dates back to the 1950s. They are not commonly used today, because they interact with many other medications, can have serious side effects, and require some dietary restrictions. For example, you cannot eat cheese or drink

* An enzyme is a chemical that builds or breaks down other chemicals.

most wines when taking these medications. These drugs interact with food and can cause severe problems with high blood pressure. They are quite effective when used under the careful guidance of a physician, however. Table 3.4 lists MAOIs by generic and trade names.

Table 3.4 Monoamine oxidase inhibitors (MAOIs)

Generic Name	Brand Name
Isocarboxazid	Marplan*
Phenelzine	Nardil
Tranylcypromine	Parnate
Selegiline	Eldepryl

*Not currently available. It was widely available until the 1990s when it was withdrawn from market by the manufacturer for unknown (possibly financial) reasons.

D. Newer Antidepressants[7]

Many of the newer antidepressant medications have vastly different molecular structures and unique chemical actions unlike those of the categories of antidepressant medications previously discussed. These are the newest antidepressants, many only recently approved for use by the federal Food and Drug Administration (FDA).

As a rule, these medications have fewer and milder side effects. Because they are new, clinicians and patients may, over time discover other side effects. Again, it is important for you to discuss possible side effects with your doctor and your pharmacist.

The development of newer antidepressant medications reflects the ongoing quest for effective, better-tolerated treatments. Table 3.5 lists medications considered "new" at the writing of this book. Fortunately, scientists continue to work on new treatments to help those who are depressed.

Table 3.5 Other antidepressants

Generic Name	Brand Name
Venlafaxine	Effexor
Mirtazapine	Remeron
Nefazodone	Serzone
Bupropion	Wellbutrin, Zyban

E. Herbals

St. John's wort (*Hypericum perforatum*) is an herbal preparation primarily studied and used in Europe. Physicians in those countries use it to treat mild and moderate forms of depressive disorders.[8] Although available in the United States, it is not currently approved by the FDA for use as an antidepressant. However, the National Institute of Mental Health (NIMH) is in the process of conducting studies to assess its effectiveness.

Many people assume that over-the-counter herbals are safe. They don't realize that they can have serious side effects. Like other medications they can interact with other medications. It is best to take St. John's wort under the guidance of a physician.

3. Therapeutic Procedures

This last category of treatments for Clinical Depression includes two therapies that use medical devices. Mental health clinicians who administer them must have special training. Both are rare, but effective, treatments for special types of Clinical Depression.

Electroconvulsive Therapy (ECT)[9, 10, 11]

Of all the therapies, electroconvulsive therapy (ECT) is, perhaps, the most widely misunderstood. There are many misconceptions about what it is and how it's used in clinical practice. Media misrepresentations showing Frankenstein-like images of this procedure add to the confusion generated by misinformation from groups seeking to discredit the entire mental health profession.

The predominant use of ECT is for prolonged severe and/or psychotic depression that fails to respond to all other treatments. Clinicians also recommend ECT for the severely depressed who can't take antidepressants for medical reasons.

As described in *Depression in Primary Care*, ECT is a " treatment usually reserved for very severe or psychotic depression, or manic states that don't respond to medication treatment. A low-voltage alternating current is sent to the brain to induce a seizure which apparently accounts for the therapeutic effect."[12] It is considered the single most effective treatment for people with severe depression who also have urgent or strong suicidal tendencies. About 80 to 85% of depressed people who receive ECT have a therapeutic response.

During ECT there is an anesthesiologist or nurse anesthetist who gives a sedative (general anesthesia) and a muscle relaxant before the treatment begins. They are in attendance at all times. A mental health physician specialist then administers a brief burst of low-voltage current through electrodes placed on one or both sides of the scalp. The person undergoing ECT is not awake and, as is the case with any general anesthesia, usually has no memory of the procedure.

The most common side effect of ECT is temporary memory impairment. Some have longer term problems with memory. The risks associated with this procedure are the same as those associated with any general anesthetic. A detailed discussion of the specific risks related to anesthesia is beyond the scope of this book and should be discussed with the doctor recommending ECT. Additionally, there are special medical conditions that rule out the use of ECT. As in the case of other treatments, all of these issues should be discussed with your doctor.

Light Therapy[13, 14]

Light Therapy is a fairly new treatment used to treat one specific condition, Seasonal Mood Disorder (SAD). Clinical studies show that it can be an effective treatment for depression with mild to moderate symptoms. As described in Chapter 2, people with this disorder experience symptoms during certain seasons of the year, typically autumn and winter.

Researchers speculate that people with SAD are unusually sensitive to the amount of sunlight in their environment. They theorize that, for some, their "biological rhythms" depend on a specific amount of light to function properly. During the fall and winter, when the number of daylight hours decreases, they become depressed because the pattern of release of brain chemicals has been altered.

In light therapy, a person sits in a room near a device formatted to deliver exceptionally bright artificial light (approximately 2,500 lux). A physician, experienced with this therapy, prescribes the exact amount of time needed for treatment, usually two to three hours a day, every day for several months. These devices are usually portable, and can be used at home or taken to the office.

HOW ARE THESE TREATMENTS USED IN CLINICAL PRACTICE?

There are three factors that determine the choice of depression treatments: the diagnosis, the level of severity, and the personal preferences of the person suffering with depression. Diagnosis refers to the specific type of Clinical Depression. As you learned in Chapter 2, this group of disorders includes several distinct clinical syndromes. Clinical Depression is a general term that refers to a wide range of clinical disorders that vary in terms of the number of symptoms experienced, the kind of symptoms, and the length of time or persistence of reported symptoms.

After diagnosis, the most crucial determinant of the available options is the severity of the disorder. Level of severity refers to whether the symptoms are mild, moderate or severe. As a general rule, the milder forms of depression have more treatment alternatives. When depression is severe the choices narrow to modalities that address serious impairment.

Personal preference is the third key factor that influences treatment selection. Although those with mild to moderate depression have more choices, even those with severe illness have a number of alternatives to consider.

The following section reviews treatment alternatives. This is an overview presented to give you general information about the clinical management of depression. We do not suggest or recommend specific therapies. Each person comes with a unique set of needs and circumstances that must be addressed. The final decision about treatment selection is a decision for you and your doctor.

TREATMENT OPTIONS[15]

Psychotherapy alone, medications alone, or a combination of the two are the typical outpatient treatment alternatives. ECT and Light Therapy are also used in outpatient settings, but only under special circumstances.

1. Psychotherapy Alone

Cognitive Behavioral Therapy and Interpersonal Therapy are both effective treatments for mild to moderate Clinical Depression. There is currently no evidence to support the use of psychodynamic therapy alone to treat depression.

To briefly review Chapter 2, people with mild depression report significant symptoms, however, they are able to make it through the day without significant impairment. This means that although they don't feel well, they can manage work and household activities with effort, but without significant impairment.

People with moderate depression have more symptoms than those with mild depression. Despite putting forth a great deal of effort, they can't function well at work or at home. They feel too ill to work and may frequently call in sick. Their lives slowly unravel as they begin having trouble taking care of themselves and their families.

Using either therapy, sufferers usually begin to notice some improvement in about six to eight weeks, but response to therapy often takes a couple of weeks longer than does response to medications. Complete resolution of symptoms may take longer as they learn to apply the techniques and suggestions learned in therapy.

2. Medication Alone

Although medications are effective treatments for mild to moderate depression, they are the standard treatment for severe depression. This is particularly true for any depression with suicidal and/or psychotic symptoms. Medications are more likely to be prescribed if the doctor is a primary care provider, because it is something that she/he can provide in their own practice and doesn't require referral to another doctor or therapist. Most primary care doctors don't provide their own psychotherapy for depression, except for the kind of general supportive therapy that is part of an overall good doctor-patient relationship or part of managing medications.

People with severe depressive disorders are usually too impaired to work. Their symptoms are so severe that they have problems doing simple things like washing and grooming themselves. When extreme, sufferers hallucinate or have bizarre ideas about others and themselves. They lose the ability to see what is real and what is not. Some become so hopeless that they decide that life is not worth living. The treatment of suicidal symptoms is discussed in the section on Special Issues in Chapter 6.

For those taking medication, symptoms typically begin to improve in about four to six weeks, as the medications start to take effect. At the same time, however, they may also experience some medication side effects. Some side effects are minor and get better or go away with time. Others are more persistent. The range of side effects depends on the specific medication.

3. Psychotherapy and Medication Combined

"I think that what has helped me is extensive counseling plus medication. I go to counseling every 2 weeks. I can honestly thank god and them for me being alive."

Using psychotherapy and medication together is probably as effective as either treatment on its own, and there is growing evidence that this combination can be better than either treatment alone.[16] Combination treatment is particularly helpful for chronic depression.

Therapies used for combination treatment include Cognitive Behavioral Therapy (CBT), Interpersonal Therapy (IPT), Psychodynamic Therapy and Supportive Therapy.

4. ECT

ECT is primarily used in two situations, (1) when severe depression does not respond to any form of medication management, and (2) when serious medical illness rules out the possibility of taking an antidepressant. Clinicians usually try several different combinations of antidepressants before considering ECT.

Outpatient ECT usually involves a series of treatments given over the course of one to two weeks. The number of treatments depends on how quickly symptoms improve. Some doctors report that ECT is particularly successful in relieving suicidal or psychotic symptoms that failed to respond to antidepressant and antipsychotic medications.[17]

When used by physicians trained in the use and delivery of this procedure, ECT can be a safe, effective treatment with few risks or side effects. As mentioned previously, the side effects include those associated with general anesthesia.

5. Light Therapy

The principal indication for Light Therapy is for mild to moderate depression with a well-documented pattern of recurrent seasonal symptoms. This treatment is frequently used in combination with antidepressant medications.

WHAT ARE THE INDICATIONS FOR HOSPITAL TREATMENT?

Sometimes Clinical Depression is so severe that sufferers cannot be adequately or safely treated in an outpatient setting. This is the case for those without hope, who believe that suicide is the only way out, and for those with psychotic thoughts, who feel compelled to hurt others. In both cases, inpatient treatment may be crucial to keeping them out of harm's way. Hospital treatment may, also, become necessary when the depressed can't function at home or become so withdrawn that they don't take care of themselves.

Suicidal thoughts

The risk of suicide in depression is high. Of patients treated in specialty clinics, about 15%, or about 1 out of every 7, will eventually kill themselves.[18] Because the danger is so great, people with suicidal thoughts need *immediate* evaluation by a healthcare professional.

Not everyone with suicidal thoughts needs immediate hospitalization. However, if the depressed go beyond just thinking about suicide and begin to make plans for ways to accomplish it, believe that suicide is the only hope for ending the suffering, and have a personal or family history of suicide or suicide attempts, hospitalization may be the only safe way to treat the depression.

Irrational thoughts about harming others

Sometimes the severely depressed begin thinking irrationally. When this happens, they begin having bizarre thoughts and paranoid suspicions about those around them. Sometimes thinking becomes so disturbed that they feel compelled to kill to protect themselves or their loved loves. In their mental confusion they believe that they are doing the right thing. These are symptoms of psychosis and also require *immediate* assessment.

When the depressed have severe psychotic symptoms that don't respond to outpatient treatment, especially when they begin to think about hurting someone, hospitalization is probably the best way to protect everyone involved.

Severe depression with complete loss of ability to function

Some people with severe depression lose almost all of their ability to function. They can't care for themselves and need someone to prompt them to feed, groom, and clothe themselves. Some lie in bed all day, others sit staring at the walls. They usually don't respond to encouragement and often resent it because they feel that others simply don't understand.

When medications don't help them improve, they may need intensive hospital care.

Hospitalization allows for close clinical observation. Clinicians provide minute-to-minute evaluation and management of dangerous symptoms. The same treatments used in outpatient settings are available in the inpatient setting; however, unless there are specific reasons not to use them, medications are almost always used. Severe symptoms sometimes require medications that can only be used in a hospital setting. ECT is both an inpatient and outpatient treatment.

Table 3.6 presents a comparison of various treatments for depression.

Table 3.6 Comparison of treatments

	Psychotherapy	Medications	ECT	Light Therapy
Appropriate for which levels of severity of Clinical Depression	Mild or moderate	All: (mild, moderate or severe)	Severe	Only used for Seasonal Affective Disorder
Cost	The exact cost to the individual depends on insurance status (whether one has health insurance) and the type of health insurance plan			
Type of trained professional who can provide treatment	Therapist (LCSW, MFCC, MFT), Psychologist (PhD), Psychiatrist (MD)	Psychiatrist (MD), Primary care clinician (MD)	Psychiatrist (MD)	Psychiatrist MD
Frequency of visits	Weekly sessions (sometimes more than once a week)	Daily medication with follow-up appointment intervals of 1-3 months depending on the rate of improvement	Individualized	Individualized
Duration of treatment	Typically 12 weeks to 1 year, but can last longer	Typically 6 months to 1 year, but can last longer	Typically weeks but can last longer	Typically weeks but can last longer
When you'll start feeling better	Responses to treatment vary by individual. See Chapter 6 for more information about the recovery process.			

CHAPTER 4

GETTING
THE BEST CARE

"I began therapy and my new medication. My first visit with the psychologist was incredible. Towards the end of that session she said to me, 'After all you have told me, it's no wonder you are sick, depressed, and having anxiety attacks.' Finally someone understood. Finally I had some support."

"What I would recommend for others in my situation is to go get help, go to mental health, tell other people your problem. If only my son would have asked for help. Instead of making people think everything was okay. He would still be alive."

The good news about Clinical Depression is that people do not have to suffer in silence or feel doomed to a life of relentless emotional pain. There are many successful treatments. Moreover, the discovery of new and better treatments continues.

After reading the previous chapters you may begin to realize that you or someone close to you suffers from Clinical Depression. This chapter is about how to get the best possible care. Step-by-step we'll guide you through the process of getting the treatment needed to recover from depression and begin enjoying life.

Getting better starts with finding the healthcare professional who can best help you. Waiting without starting treatment increases the chances that the symptoms will worsen and become more severe. If you do not already have a family doctor, or if you do not see anyone for routine medical care, finding someone to work with you is key. Even a regular doctor may not ensure that you get the best care.

Although this book provides you with information about the many signs and symptoms of depression, it cannot take the place of a thorough assessment by a trained healthcare professional. It is *very important* that anyone with depressive symptoms see a doctor, someone experienced in diagnosing and treating Clinical Depression.

WHO TREATS CLINICAL DEPRESSION?

There are two basic categories of healthcare practitioners who diagnose and treat Clinical Depression: Primary Care Clinicians and Mental Health Specialists. These groups are further divided into those who prescribe medications, those who provide psychotherapy, and those who can provide both treatment modalities.

Primary Care Clinicians provide comprehensive medical care. Another term for a Primary Care Doctor is "Family Doctor" or "General Practitioner." Nurse Practitioners are Registered Nurses with additional training in medical diagnosis and treatment. They can also deliver primary care. Primary care is the overall healthcare to prevent illness and maintain your health across physical and emotional health concerns. The primary care specialties include Family Practice, Internal Medicine, Pediatrics, and Gynecology.

Mental Health specialties include Psychiatry, Psychology, and Social Work. Some states* license another category of counselor— Marriage, Family, and Child Counselors (MFCC) or Marriage and Family Therapists (MFT)—to provide therapy. All licensed Mental

* California, for example.

Health Specialists have special training in psychotherapy. Because Cognitive Behavioral Therapy and Interpersonal Therapy require additional training, not all Mental Health Specialists can offer these treatments.

A psychiatrist is a medical doctor (M.D.) with specialty training in the diagnosis and treatment of emotional and mental disorders. Like other medical doctors, they can prescribe medications and, when necessary, admit patients to the hospital. In most states, psychiatrists or neurologists are the only specialists who can administer ECT.

Clinical psychologists have doctoral level training (a Ph.D.) in the diagnosis and treatment of emotional and mental disorders. They have special training in psychological testing, tools used to assess emotional, behavioral, and learning difficulties. As a general rule, psychologists are not licensed to prescribe medications or admit to the hospital.

Social workers work in many areas of healthcare, including mental health. There are three educational degrees in social work: Licensed Clinical Social Work (L.C.S.W.), Masters in Social Work (M.S.W.), and Doctoral Degree in Social Work (Ph.D.) In addition to psychotherapy, social workers have training in the assessment of individual and family problems related to welfare, homelessness, or other resource issues.

Part of the process of finding care is evaluating any obstacles to your full participation in an ongoing treatment plan. Financial considerations, problems arranging time off from work, worry about finding someone to watch the children, and overcoming family resistance to getting help for emotional problems are some of the things that make getting regular care difficult. The next section helps you identify possible barriers and gives suggestions on how to overcome them.

STEP 1. ASSESSING ANY BARRIERS TO GETTING CARE

A. Insurance Status

To a large extent, your health insurance status will determine where you go for care and what type of clinician you see. Insurance status means whether you have health insurance and, if so, the type of coverage provided by your particular plan. Because of the special importance of health insurance to people's ability to get care, we discuss it in detail.

1. If you don't have health insurance...

Most states provide a publicly funded healthcare system for those who don't have the financial resources to pay for needed health care. If you do not have health insurance, one of the first things to do is investigate your community healthcare resources. Your area may have state or county clinics where you can register for state or federally subsidized care.

Some public hospitals also provide outpatient care through a network of ambulatory care clinics. The yellow pages of the telephone directory almost always list city, county, and state healthcare facilities in your area. If not, call information to get the telephone number of your county or state health department. They should be able to direct you to the facility nearest you. Male and female veterans are eligible for care at federally funded Veterans Administration healthcare facilities. Local veterans' organizations can provide information about the location of VA hospitals and clinics.

The county and state health departments are also a good source of information about eligibility criteria for state and federal health insurance programs. Depending on your finances, you may qualify for Medicaid (the state program) or Medicare (the federal program which covers people with disabilities and those aged 65 or older). Medicaid coverage varies by state. Most states provide at least some coverage for mental health services, although not all do.

If you have children at home, you may qualify for *Healthy Families*, or *State Children's Health Insurance* (S-CHIP), a relatively new federal/state partnership program that, like Medicaid, covers different healthcare services, depending on the state.

In addition to publicly funded facilities, some communities have privately funded, non-profit clinics that offer reduced fees for those with financial need who don't qualify for state or federal programs. Some areas have special programs to help pay for the costs of prescription medications. Some clinics have a "sliding scale" fee schedule, where individuals are charged only what they can afford to pay, usually based on a pre-defined set of rules for payment.

2. If you do have health insurance...

There are two basic types of private health insurance: fee-for-service and managed care. Some plans offer elements of both. Almost all elderly people in the United States have Medicare, which is a federal health-insurance program with two major components: Part A, which is mandatory, and Part B, which is optional and provides additional coverage. Medicare is designed as a fee-for-service plan, but there are also managed care plans that carry contracts with Medicare. People on Medicare can also have supplemental private insurance, which then acts like any other private health-insurance plan which means that the private insurance pays a portion (or all) of the costs not covered by Medicare.

Fee-for-service insurance plans usually do not limit an enrollee's choice of clinicians or facilities that provide care. Using standard guidelines for provider training and licensing, they reimburse care chosen by the client. The insured pay a fixed percent, or amount of costs, after a predetermined yearly premium for the insurance, which may be paid by them or their employer. Most private insurance is through employment.

When planning to get care for depression, it is important to anticipate that you may have insurance coverage for mental-health care that is less generous than you are used to based on your experience with your general medical care. You can look at your insurance policy and the summary in your booklet or on your insurance card. Insurance policies have been changing rapidly lately, so make sure you have the current information. The costs you face for mental health care, if you have a fee-for-service insurance plan, will depend on your exact type of coverage.

Care for depression—particularly hospitalization and some prescribed medications—can be expensive. It is important to treat depression early before it becomes so severe that the higher level of care you require might exceed what your insurance plan covers.

Sometimes plans also exclude coverage for pre-existing conditions. This means that if you've had a problem before, your insurance might not cover the benefits for care for the same conditions when you sign up for a new plan. This can happen with both mental and physical disorders. Sometimes you can still be covered for a prior condition, but have to pay more for the coverage. It's important to consider this feature when signing up for a plan. If you have already signed up for a plan that you expect to stay with for some time, this is not likely to be a problem at the point that you start care.

Managed care is the second type of insurance plan today. Managed care is called that because the plans and practices use different types of "management" approaches to keep the costs of healthcare low. Managed care also uses administrative and clinical oversight or care, which is sometimes also referred to as case management. Under these procedures, doctors or patients have to receive approval for the care that is delivered. Some insurance plans offer a combination of elements from both fee-for-service and managed care. Some fee-for-service plans offer a list of preferred providers and hospitals.

Managed-care plans generally pay for all authorized care after the co-payment. The insured who choose clinicians outside of the preferred list generally pay a larger percent of their healthcare costs.

For either fee-for-service or managed care, it's important for you to understand what your plan covers. You need to:

1. Review your insurance plan. List the different costs to you of receiving mental-health care. Obtain a list of the specialists who can provide mental-health care for your plan. Check whether you need prior approval.

2. Review your choice of clinicians covered by your plan.

B. Work Issues

Getting healthcare takes time. If your job doesn't allow time for medical care or sick leave, there may be other ways of arranging time off for a medical visit. One possibility is adjusting your work hours (for example, coming in later and leaving later) on the day of your appointment so that you don't lose pay. Discussing scheduling options with your boss or supervisor is one way to begin. An alternative is to find clinics that have evening or weekend hours or that can schedule appointments when you are free.

In the Partners in Care study, we found that patients who received good quality care for depression were more likely to have jobs than patients who did not.* Researchers learned that one im-

---

* At the 18 month point in the Partners in Care study, patients who visited practices with special programs to improve the quality of care for Clinical Depression were more likely to have jobs than those in clinics without the special programs.

portant effect of improving the quality of care for depression is improving the stability of employment. Good care helps rather than harms the chances for getting and keeping a job.

C. Family Attitudes and/or Cultural Beliefs

"Do not let social taboos dissuade you from seeking help. Allow yourself to be human. There are upwards of five billion people on this planet and every single one of us has feet of clay. Be at least as good to yourself as you are to others."

Family members or people from your cultural, racial, ethnic, or social community may have beliefs or attitudes that make you reluctant to seek medical treatment. They may even think that emotional issues should not be discussed outside of the family. There are still many people who don't understand that depression is a **medical** illness, one that affects millions of people each year. Seeking treatment is a sign of strength, not weakness. As friends and family see you improve, their opinions will probably change.

As you learned in Chapter 1, there are many myths about depression. These misconceptions cause some people to have unhelpful attitudes or unrealistic ideas about this kind of emotional distress. It may be hard for your family, or you, to accept that you have depression. Accurate information is the best way to overcome these kinds of misunderstandings.

D. Childcare

Having young children in the examining room can interfere with your ability to talk openly with your doctor. The person evaluating you may need to ask very personal questions. You may need to discuss problems that are not appropriate for your children to hear. Most medical offices don't have the facilities to provide childcare during your office visit. Asking a trusted friend or family member to go with you to watch your children while you talk with the doctor is one way to get help. Still, taking your children with you to the doctor's office is better than not getting care.

E. Transportation

Getting to routine office visits will be a challenge if you don't drive a car and don't live in an area with good public transportation. Your community may have resources to help you get to medical appointments. There may be non-profit organizations that provide van transportation or taxi vouchers. Contacting your local social service agency is one way to investigate the possibilities.

Helping with transportation is one way that your family and friends can assist you in starting and keeping with a treatment plan. Although the early phases of depression treatment may be the time when you need the most help finding ways to get to your clinical visits, as you improve, you will be able to take over solving these kinds of problems.

F. No Local Healthcare Facility

If you live in a rural or remote area where there are no healthcare facilities and no doctors, finding care will be more of a challenge. Some states and counties fly doctors to isolated areas to conduct medical clinics at regular intervals.

Some medical centers provide care "at a distance" through a system called Telemedicine. Telemedicine doctors use video or telephone conferencing to speak with patients. Pharmacists mail prescriptions to those requiring medications. Contacting your state or county health department is a way to find out if your state provides this kind of care. Friends in your area can also share strategies for how they got care.

G. Language Issues (Including Deafness)

For some, language is a significant barrier. This includes sign language. Finding a clinic with healthcare providers who speak your language is not always easy. Some facilities have interpreters trained to translate in healthcare settings. Many centers that don't have trained personnel have staff who can speak your language and communicate your concerns. Asking about interpreter services before making an appointment will help you get that need met.

Reviewing Barriers

Table 4.1 lists some problems that can make getting treatment difficult. This list is based on the kinds of barriers reported by the patients participating in the RAND Partners in Care study. Review this list and check off any conditions that apply to you. Be sure to add problems affecting you that are not on the list. Share the list of barriers with your doctor or loved ones, so that they can help.

Table 4.1 What things would make it harder for me to get care?

Which of the following reasons would make it difficult for you to get care?

1. I worry about cost.	YES	NO
2. The clinician won't accept my health insurance.	YES	NO
3. My health plan won't pay for my treatment.	YES	NO
4. I can't find where to go for help.	YES	NO
5. I can't get an appointment as soon as I need one.	YES	NO
6. I can't get to the clinician's office when it's open.	YES	NO
7. It takes too long to get to the clinician's office from my house or work.	YES	NO
8. I can't get through on the telephone or leave messages.	YES	NO
9. I don't think I can be helped.	YES	NO

Table 4.1 What things would make it harder for me to get care? (Cont.)

10. I am too embarrassed to discuss my problem with anyone.	YES	NO
11. I am afraid of what others will think of me.	YES	NO
12. I can't get work leave for medical appointments and will lose pay.	YES	NO
13. I need someone to take care of my children.	YES	NO
14. No one speaks my language at the clinician's office.	YES	NO
15. I feel discriminated against because of my age, race, ethnicity, or sexual orientation.	YES	NO

STEP 2. GETTING A CLINICAL EVALUATION AND DIAGNOSIS

"[Getting treatment was] a big help to me in helping me talk about my problems and worries. It helped me open up more to my family and I was able to recognize they were there to support me for as long as it took to get back to helping them."

In many ways this is the hardest step. Talking about personal feelings is never easy, and is especially difficult when you're feeling sad or hopeless. Depression is a profoundly disabling illness. It can sap your energy; making it almost impossible to do the things that will help you get better. Even if you already have a family doctor, this task can seem overwhelming.

There is a Chinese proverb that says, "The journey begins with the first step." In the case of Clinical Depression, the journey to relief begins with finding a clinician to assess you and determine whether you have Clinical Depression.

For most people, the first person they will see at a public or private clinic is a Primary Care Clinician, someone trained to provide comprehensive medical care. As you learned in Chapter 2, depressive symptoms can indicate other medical illnesses besides Clinical Depression. For this reason, it is important to get a thorough medical evaluation before beginning any treatment regimen. This evaluation should include a complete physical examination with screening blood work to rule out other diseases.

As a general rule, doctors will ask you about any troubling symptoms before performing a physical examination. It is important that you mention everything that bothers you, including when your symptoms began and whether your feelings affect your ability to work or enjoy social activities. One of the best ways to ensure that you mention everything is to write down your key symptoms and problems on a sheet of paper.

Table 4.2 gives a sample of the kind of list you should make. You will find the same list in the Appendix at the end of the book. There is space to add any symptoms that you don't see on the list. Copy, photocopy, or remove the page, then check the column(s) next to the symptoms you experience. A sheet for listing any current medications appears on page 186 of the Appendix. Bring the completed sheets with you to your medical visit. The list will help you remember what you need to tell your doctor.

Table 4.2 Feelings that I'm experiencing

✔	Key Symptoms and Problems
	I feel sad or "empty" almost all of the time.
	I don't have interest in things that I used to find enjoyable, like sex, sports, reading, or listening to music.
	I have trouble concentrating, thinking, remembering, or making decisions.
	I have trouble falling asleep, staying asleep or sleeping too much.
	I've noticed a loss of energy and feel tired.

Table 4.2 Feelings that I'm experiencing (Cont.)

I'm noticing a change in my eating pattern with either a loss of appetite or eating much more than usual.
I'm losing or gaining weight without trying.
I cry or feel like crying a lot.
I feel irritable or "on edge" a lot.
I feel worthless or guilty a lot.
I feel hopeless or pessimistic most of the time.
I think a lot about death, including thoughts about suicide.
I have frequent headaches, body aches, and pains.
I have stomach and digestive trouble with bowel irregularity.

You will also need to inform your doctor about any past treatments for depression. Providing a list of all previous treatment and medications will help in making the decision about which treatment course to begin.

In Partners in Care, study participants used checklists of symptoms similar to the one in Chapter 1. This helped them explain symptoms to their doctors.

After taking a history of your symptoms, your doctor should perform a routine physical examination and order screening tests, which may include laboratory work, a chest X-ray, and a cardiogram. Request an internal exam (pelvic for women, rectal for men) if you have not had a medical evaluation in more than a year.

At the end of your medical evaluation, your doctor will talk about any physical findings and discuss whether your symptoms indicate Clinical Depression.* If the answer is "yes," the next step is reviewing available treatments and determining a course of action.

* Laboratory results may modify or change the preliminary diagnosis.

STEP 3. WORKING WITH YOUR DOCTOR TO CHOOSE THE BEST TREATMENT REGIMEN

"I am extremely fortunate in having a loving, caring family. . . and a very understanding PAC [Primary Care Clinician]. She is a wonderful listener and has become a good friend. When I became more concerned about my mental-health condition, she explained to me in detail about prescribing an antidepressant."

Unfortunately, getting the diagnosis of Clinical Depression does not ensure that you will get the best possible care. Much depends on the type of clinician treating you and the mental health resources in your community, as well as your own initiative and persistence, as you've seen in the letters in this book.

Primary Care Clinicians vary in their level of comfort and expertise in prescribing antidepressant medications. Also, clinicians occasionally differ in their personal opinions about the effectiveness of some treatments. This is especially true in the case of psychotherapy. Many outside of the field of mental health have little or no information about the role of psychotherapy as treatment for depression. They may not know that structured psychotherapies are as effective as medications in treating most types of depression that are treated on an outpatient basis.

A recent national study found that people with Clinical Depression in treatment with general medical doctors were less likely to receive appropriate care than those treated by mental-health specialists.[1] This does not mean that you won't get good care if you see a primary care doctor. There are primary care doctors who successfully treat depression. This finding does suggest that, when possible, you should select your clinician very carefully. Make sure that your clinician is aware of your symptoms and has access to good information on treating depression.

There is information about the kind of care that ensures good treatment. The Partners in Care research study worked with patients and primary care doctors to identify ways to improve depression care in general medical settings. Researchers identified several components of care that enhanced the quality. Educating patients about depression was one important element. Researchers prepared special materials, including booklets and a video, which explained Clinical Depression and discussed treatment.

People with depression can have problems remembering appointments and often struggle when trying to manage their own care. For this reason another key ingredient of the study was the role of the nurse care coordinator. A nurse, functioning in this capacity, helped participants prepare for medical visits by helping them review and list their symptoms. As the care coordinator, this nurse also helped them think about their treatment preferences and coached them in ways to raise this issue with the doctor. The coordinator also kept track of scheduled office visits and contacted participants who missed appointments. They followed how treatments affected people, including side effects, and relayed problems to the doctor.

If the system or medical practice where you go for care doesn't have a nurse or other clinical person who can help you in the way that nurse coordinators functioned in the Partners in Care study, there may still be ways to incorporate some of the things they did into your treatment regimen. Your doctor may be able to provide someone who can remind you of appointments by telephoning you or mailing postcard reminders. If not, you could ask a good friend, spouse, or roommate to help remind you of appointments.

Working with an experienced clinician, one familiar with diagnosing and treating depression, is crucial to receiving the appropriate medication and getting a timely referral to a mental health specialist when needed.

> *". . . Gone are those lonely and protracted days and weeks of depression. And I am convinced that if I had not learned how and what to ask and/or to state to my doctors I would still be in the same boat I was four or five years ago."*

A. Investigating the Available Treatments

Chapter 3 discussed the standard treatments for Clinical Depression and briefly reviewed their use in clinical practice. Each of these treatments (medications, psychotherapy, and procedures) can be used alone or in combination, depending on each person's specific symptoms. The treatments described in that chapter are evidence-based treatments, meaning that solid clinical research confirms their effectiveness.

Chapter 3 also described how the severity of symptoms impacts treatment choice. To briefly review, in most cases, treatment with psychotherapy alone is an alternative only for those with mild to moderate symptoms. Medication management is an option for all levels of severity, including mild to moderate depression. Combination treatment is also an option for all levels of severity. Returning to Chapter 3 can help you review this issue.

Healthcare resources vary widely from community to community, however. Depending on where you live and your health insurance, the full range of evidence-based treatments may not be available to you. In reality, your particular treatment options depend not only on your preferences and the severity of your symptoms, but also on your community's healthcare resources.

Although some hospitals and insurance plans restrict the antidepressants that they provide,* most antidepressant medications are widely available. This is not the case for the two psychotherapies shown to effectively treat Clinical Depression. Cognitive Behavioral Therapy (CBT) and Interpersonal Therapy (IPT) require therapists to undertake additional training and certification. Both are treatments that use special protocols. The psychotherapists in your area may not have CBT or IPT training. However, getting some form of psychotherapy may still be a possibility, even if your doctor cannot locate a CBT or IPT therapist.

Psychiatrists, psychologists, and most other mental-health specialists receive training in supportive and psychodynamic therapy. Future research may show these other therapies to be helpful in treating depression. Many therapists use techniques similar to those used in CBT and IPT. However, CBT and IPT are currently the only two forms of psychotherapy recommended for use without medications.

B. Reviewing Your Preferences

People with depression, especially those with severe symptoms, can feel overwhelmed at the thought of having to make a decision about treatment. Making choices is difficult when a person has trouble concentrating or feels hopeless.

After reading through the chapter on depression treatments, however, you may discover that you feel more comfortable starting psychotherapy or medication. Combination treatment may be your preferred choice. If so, your doctor needs to know how you feel. Open communication is essential to finding the right regimen. If you don't have a strong preference, then you can decide on the

---

* Some Managed Care Organizations restrict their drug formularies to certain medications.

basis of what fits best into your life, the costs, or even your doctor's preference.

You may also have an opinion about who treats your depression, including the person who prescribes your medications. If you would prefer to see a psychiatrist for medications, and your health plan allows you that choice, mention this to the doctor. It is vital that you work with someone you trust.

If you are concerned, there are ways to talk about these issues without sounding discourteous or antagonistic. Table 4.3 gives some examples. If you feel too uneasy or uncomfortable, you might ask a trusted friend or family member to accompany you to the visit and participate in the discussion. A caring clinician will always appreciate your input.

Table 4.3 Sample questions for working with your doctor to determine your preferences and decide who treats your depression

If your options and preferences include medication alone:	"Doctor X, will you prescribe my antidepressant medications or will you refer me to a psychiatrist for medication management?"
If your options and preferences include psychotherapy alone:	"If possible, I would like to try psychotherapy before considering medications. I've read about two special therapies for people with Clinical Depression. Are there therapists in my community who can provide these particular treatments?"
	Note: If the answer is "no," you need to decide whether you would still like to pursue psychotherapy alone or in combination with medications.
If your options and preferences include combination treatment:	"I would like to try both medication and psychotherapy. Is there a way to arrange for me to get both treatments?"

Tables 4.4 and 4.5 review your treatment history and prompt you to think about your treatment preferences.

Table 4.4 Experience and attitudes about depression treatment

As you and your doctor discuss treatment options, it's important to talk about your past experiences with depression treatment(s), including those of family members.

Have you been diagnosed with depression in the past?	YES	NO
If yes, did you receive any form of treatment?	YES	NO
Have you ever taken antidepressant medications?	YES	NO
If yes, were they helpful?	YES	NO
Have any family or friends taken antidepressant medications?	YES	NO
If yes, were they helpful?	YES	NO
Have you ever tried counseling or therapy?	YES	NO
If yes, was it helpful?	YES	NO
Have any family or friends tried counseling or therapy?	YES	NO
If yes, was it helpful?	YES	NO
Are you against taking medications? If yes, why?	YES	NO
Are you against counseling or therapy? If yes, why?	YES	NO

Table 4.5 What are my personal depression treatment preferences?*

✔	Options and preferences
	Psychotherapy alone (for those with mild to moderate symptoms only)
	Medication alone (for those with mild, moderate, or severe symptoms)
	Combination treatment—medication and psychotherapy (for those with mild, moderate, or severe symptoms)

*If all are indicated, and available.

STEP 4. BEGINNING TREATMENT: WHAT TO EXPECT

"When can I expect to start feeling better?" is one of the first questions asked when starting treatment for depression. Even though the precise amount of time it takes to recover from depression varies, there are general guidelines for how long each treatment should take. Like most other medical illnesses, full recovery may take several weeks.

A. Psychotherapy Alone

People with mild to moderate symptoms who get weekly Cognitive Behavioral or Interpersonal Therapy generally start to notice some improvement in about six to eight weeks. Their mood gradually lifts. They start feeling better about themselves and more hopeful about the future. Complete recovery usually takes several more weeks.

Some therapists feel that other forms of therapy also can help with depression. However, research studies have not yet confirmed the effectiveness of other therapies. Because of this, it is best to be cautious in choosing any treatment that is not standard.

For any form of psychotherapy, if by 12 weeks you notice only slight improvement, or if your symptoms have not improved at all, medication may be the next step.

To have a good chance of obtaining the benefit from psychotherapy, you need to do your best to follow through with appointments and recommendations.

B. Medications

"I now have chosen to take medication. I do not want to have to take meds, but it's easier to get through the days."

People taking medications usually start feeling better in about four to six weeks. Medications are especially effective in managing problems with sleep, appetite, and energy level. These are some of the first symptoms to improve. As the weeks progress, people feel less downhearted and more optimistic about life getting back to normal.

All medications carry the risk of drug interactions and side effects. Some side effects are minor and go away with time. Others are more serious and need immediate medical attention. Although not everyone taking antidepressants experiences side effects, each person needs this kind of information about their particular medication(s) to prepare them in the event that they do.

Make sure that you have a clear understanding of the dose, the timing, and possible side effects. You need to know how many pills you should take each day, the exact time for taking each one, and important warning signs. Discuss this with your doctor and ask for material to take home to help you remember what to look for. Many medical offices and pharmacies provide patient information sheets with detailed information. A list of some additional resources appears on page 177.

As with therapy, you may well need help to take medications in the way that your doctor prescribed. Talk to your doctor and pharmacist to make sure that you know the exact amounts and times for taking your pills. Alert your doctor about any side effects. Don't stop taking the medication without his/her approval.

"What's funny now is that I feel better than I ever did before I got sick. I have made many positive changes in my life and somehow I feel stronger than I was before my depression. Will the depression ever come again? I hope not, but I know if it does, I'll be ready for it."

CHAPTER 5

TEN THINGS I CAN DO TO HELP MYSELF

It's hard to think about doing anything when you're feeling demoralized and weak. Even small changes can provide significant benefits, however. In addition to getting clinical treatment, there are many things that you can do to help yourself. This chapter discusses ten of them. These are simple, uncomplicated techniques that can, over time, assist the process of your recovery. However, they should complement, not replace, good clinical care.

If you are severely depressed and feel that you don't have the energy to undertake any of the things discussed here, waiting until your depression begins to respond to treatment may be the best course of action. But, if you can find it within yourself to try some of these suggestions, there is a good chance that you'll find them beneficial.

There are times when you need to ask a friend or family member to lend a hand. Asking for help is never easy and can be particularly difficult when you're depressed. In Chapter 7 there is a special section on talking with family and friends about your depression. Clinical Depression also impacts those who care about you.

TEN THINGS I CAN DO TO HELP MYSELF

1. Have a regular bedtime

Sleep disruption is one of the most common and troubling symptoms of Clinical Depression. Even those with mild depression can experience difficulty getting to sleep and find that they awaken throughout the night. In the early phases of depression some think that insomnia is the major problem and think that their fatigue and lack of energy are a result of not getting enough rest. Some go to the drug store to get an over-the-counter preparation or ask their doctors for a sleep medication. Others just hope they'll get better with time. This symptom rarely improves by itself, and sleep medications are only a temporary solution. They don't treat the underlying condition and carry the real risk of physical and psychological addiction.

Fortunately, insomnia usually responds well to depression treatment. As the depression clears, sleep improves. However, it may take several weeks before you begin to notice the effects of treatment. As you learned in Chapter 4, both psychotherapy and medication can take from four to six weeks to begin relieving symptoms. In the period before you begin to notice improvement, there is a technique that can help with falling asleep. It is having a regular bedtime and before-sleep routine.

This may seem peculiar to those who delay going to bed until they feel extremely tired in hope of increasing their chances of falling asleep. Some fear that an earlier bedtime will mean tossing and turning for longer periods.

A regular bedtime and sleep routine, though, is a way of signaling the body that it's time to rest. It is a practice that, over time, prepares the body for sleep. The exact hour does not matter as much as lying down at approximately the same time each night. This habit conditions the body for sleep.

A bedtime ritual also helps. This can be as simple as a nightly bath or sipping a warm glass of milk. Reading or watching television in bed is not good for those who have trouble falling asleep. Both activities require a level of alertness that can make it difficult for the mind to calm down. Resting quietly in a darkened room is best.

This same kind of conditioning happens to anyone who needs to get up at the same time each morning to make it to work or school on time. Initially, they may need to set an alarm. After a while, though, they usually find themselves waking automatically, often before the alarm. The daily routine trained them.

Those in treatment who have severe insomnia that doesn't respond to treatment or these techniques should talk with their doctor. Sometimes a brief trial of sleep medication can help during the period of reassessment. The treatment may need to be changed or modified.

2. Get daily, moderate exercise

*"My solution to being depressed is to join a ballroom dance class. . .
it gives a reason to get dressed up, get out of the house. People may be
scared, may have sad faces, but with laughter over learning, the sound of
music—I've seen such changes."*

There are numerous reports demonstrating that routine exercise can improve mood.[1] But, busy schedules make it difficult, sometimes impossible, to find the time. Even in the best circumstances, starting a new fitness regimen takes effort. Joining a gym or participating in a fitness class may feel uncomfortable or too expensive.

You can increase your physical activity without making elaborate preparations or spending large amounts of money and time. There is research showing that even small amounts of time (as little as twenty minutes, three times a week) are enough to increase overall physical fitness.[2]

One of the easiest ways to exercise is to walk. Racing around at a fast pace isn't necessary. Walking at a speed that doesn't tire you or leave you breathless is fine.

If you don't like walking there are many other activities. Gardening, swimming, and bicycling are other ways to become more active. Finding the time and doing it regularly is what's important.

Finding an exercise partner or a group can help those of you who don't like exercising alone. Many community and senior citizen centers coordinate walking groups and provide contact telephone numbers for local groups.

Before starting any exercise routine you must check with your doctor. A good time to talk about this is when you get your physical exam. Make sure that you also discuss the appropriate exercises for your age, weight, and physical condition.

3. Manage stress

There is no way to avoid all the stress of everyday living. Life today is very busy and most people need to juggle several responsibilities. Even those who don't work outside the home face the challenge of trying to coordinate many things to keep personal and family life in order.

Although people respond differently to strain and hardship, being alone or without emotional support, struggling with limited finances, living in poverty, enduring troubled family or work relationships, and suffering with serious medical problems are some of the things that can crush anyone's spirits. When circumstances are bad, stress can become a serious enough problem to negatively impact general health and well-being.

The worry and anxiety that accompany difficult life situations can increase the risk of developing depression. In fact, the illness often starts during the most emotionally vulnerable times. For those with Clinical Depression, the illness is an additional burden.

Most people don't have the means to change their immediate circumstances. Even if they could, there are usually no simple or quick solutions to troubling conditions. The primary goal of stress management practices is to develop constructive ways to respond to difficult situations. The following section discusses techniques and practices that can help.

A. Spiritual Practice

Many find that spiritual faith sustains and comforts them through difficult times. Following a spiritual tradition is an essential part of their lives. They may, or may not, belong to a traditional religion.* Regular participation in religious services is their way of decreasing anxiety and maintaining hope. For them, integrating religious practice into their treatment program is key to helping decrease the stress associated with having Clinical Depression. Sharing concerns about the illness with a caring spiritual advisor can ease worry. Religious practice can work in harmony with any depression treatment.

Sadly, there are times when the unrelenting hopelessness of Clinical Depression erodes spiritual belief and causes it to waver. Some fear that they are losing their faith and experience tremendous guilt and shame. If this is true for you, talking with your spiritual advisor and getting additional spiritual support can help you maintain hope. Most traditional religions offer some form of pastoral counseling to help those in need.

* Christianity, Judaism, Islam, Buddhism, Hinduism, etc.

B. Relaxation Techniques

"My counselor started me on relaxation exercises. At first I didn't believe that they could help. . . . Was it easy, no! It was [hard] and I fell backwards more than I could count."

There are several relaxation techniques that can help with managing stress. Biofeedback*, hypnosis, yoga, and massage are four techniques that can help decrease stress. However, they require that you work with certified practitioners.

Other, less technical practices that you can try on your own include listening to relaxation audiotapes, warm baths, stretching exercises, and deep breathing exercises. These techniques increase the feeling of relaxation by relieving the muscle tension that accompanies stress.

Most libraries and bookstores carry self-help books and audiotapes that describe how to do relaxation exercises. Your local librarian or bookstore clerk can help you locate them. The Internet is another source for information (see healthy.net or yourhealth.com).

Sometimes the stress and anxiety are so overwhelming that none of these techniques work. In this case, one of the more technical interventions mentioned may help. Talk with your therapist or doctor about referral to a qualified person.

4. Avoid being alone for long periods

"I cope by taking drawing lessons, exercise classes, volunteering at an elementary school. . . I suggest people push themselves into activity but know how to enjoy a quiet moment."

Depression is an illness that can cause a tremendous sense of loneliness and isolation. Many withdraw and stay away from friends and

---

*"Biofeedback is a technique in which electronic equipment is used to enable a person to monitor his or her stress responses so that he or she can modify them. In hypnosis, a practitioner uses words and suggestions to help the client reach a deep state of relaxation. Some practitioners train clients in self-hypnosis." [Modified definition from *The Oxford English Dictionary*. See the OED. 2/e. on-line version, 2002 (oed.com).]

loved ones because they feel so awful. For them, interacting with others is too painful to bear. Even those with outgoing, fun-loving personalities experience dramatic changes in the way they relate. They avoid those they care about and choose to stay by themselves. Spending long periods alone is not good and can make the situation worse. When depressed people isolate themselves, they may risk becoming even more depressed.

Research looking at people with depression found that those who had poor social support carried a greater risk of having depression. Socially isolated people tended to experience more depressive symptoms.[3]

For those with mild to moderate symptoms, becoming more socially active can help the recovery process. This doesn't mean doing activities that cause more stress. Doing simple things that don't require a lot of energy or effort are best. Going to a movie or concert with friends, attending a religious service, or meeting someone for coffee or dinner are some of the things that you can do.

Some people enjoy volunteering for community organizations. They find that helping others lifts their mood and makes life more meaningful. Again, avoid taking on tasks that make life more difficult. Many areas have "walks" that raise money for various diseases and charities. There are walks for breast cancer, AIDS, multiple sclerosis, diabetes and many other medical conditions. They are one way to be with people while doing something that is important to you. For those who enjoy athletic activities, participating in sports is another way to socialize.

Self-help groups can also give social support. There are organizations for the depressed that provide information and conduct support groups for those coping and living with depression. Membership in these groups is usually free of charge. The National Depressive and Manic Depressive Association (NDMDA) is one of these organizations, but there are others. These organizations also provide support groups for friends and family of the depressed. A list of some resources that offer these services is provided on page 177. In addition to providing information about mental health, some of these organizations advocate for research and public policy positions.

For those with severe depression, the situation is somewhat different. They often have trouble managing simple daily tasks. In that state, socializing is usually beyond their capacities. They also need a social support system, but it's to help with things like buying groceries and remembering clinic appointments. Family and friends need to become more involved in the tasks of their daily lives.

If you are depressed and live by yourself; if you don't have friends or family nearby, talk with your therapist or doctor. They may be able to suggest ways for you to find people and activities to keep you in contact with others who can help you.

When the hopelessness of depression turns into thoughts of suicide and death, being alone is dangerous. The risk of suicide is much higher for those who live alone and have no social support. When someone with suicidal thoughts begins to think and plan ways to kill themselves, the situation is a true emergency. They need immediate medical help.

If you have serious thoughts about killing yourself and have gone so far as to make plans and cannot get to a doctor, call 911 or go immediately to the nearest emergency room for help.

5. Keep scheduled appointments

Regular visits are an integral part of any treatment plan. Your doctor or therapist needs to see you to assess your progress and evaluate whether any part of your regimen needs modifying. This is particularly true if you are taking medications. If you have troubling side effects and if your symptoms show little improvement, your doctor may need to adjust your dose or change your medication.

Keeping scheduled appointments would seem to be an easy task. For people with Clinical Depression, it is not. Because of problems with concentration, many have trouble remembering dates and times. This, added to symptoms of fatigue and low motivation, make it a challenge to get regular care.

Here are some things that you can do besides relying on your memory to keep appointments. Doing some, or all, of the following things can help. They are:

1. Make appointments at times that are convenient for you.

2. Keep a calendar or appointment book with you at all times.

3. Leave a note on your refrigerator or mirror listing upcoming appointments.

4. Ask your doctor's or therapist's office to call you or send a post-card reminder listing the dates and times for appointments.

5. Ask a friend or family member to keep a duplicate copy of your schedule so that they can remind you about clinic appointments.

6. Make work-leave arrangements well ahead of scheduled appointment times so that you don't have to worry about asking for time-off at the last minute.

You may have other ideas. Making sure that you don't miss any aspect of care is vital to your recovery.

6. Record and report all medication side effects

"I have to work on taking my medications faithfully and being aware that the black cloud can come anytime, taking one day at a time."

Successful medication management requires that both you and your doctor pay close attention to any and all side effects. As mentioned in the previous section, if your symptoms don't improve, or if you experience severe side effects, your doctor may need to change you to another antidepressant regimen.

Keep a list of possible side effects for your medications. If your doctor or pharmacist doesn't have a brochure or pamphlet with this information, ask them to make a list for you. The Appendix of this book provides a sample blank sheet that your doctor or pharmacist can use.

7. Eat a healthy diet

Proper nutrition is one of the most important building blocks of good physical and emotional health. A nutritious diet can aid recuperation. People with Clinical Depression can experience a significant change in their appetite. Losing or gaining a significant amount of weight over a short period of time is common. In either case, eating nourishing food can help keep the body in balance as it begins to heal.

Information about ways to construct a healthy diet is available from the United States Department of Health and Human Services (DHHS). DHHS publishes brochures giving dietary guidelines and offers them free to the public. The Internet is another way to find information about the building blocks of a healthy diet. You will find these and other sources listed in the Depression Resources section.

8. Avoid taking on new or difficult tasks at work or at home

One of the early symptoms of depression is difficulty concentrating and paying attention. Many depressed people stop reading or watching television because they have trouble focusing on the information at hand. Taking on something new or difficult requires a level of effort and attention that is beyond the capacity of most people with Clinical Depression. Because the level of stress increases with each added responsibility, they avoid activities that take extra effort. Those doing dangerous work, where even a minor lapse of attention risks severe injury, need to take special care.

Until symptoms improve and the depression lifts, it is best to avoid any new responsibilities. This is especially true if you do hazardous work. After recovery, you will probably find it easier to take on more difficult tasks. In the meantime, you may want to discuss the situation with your boss or supervisor. If needed, your doctor or therapist can help you explain your situation to your manager. Chapter 7 discusses ways to do this.

9. Follow doctor and therapist recommendations

"After a couple months of weekly therapy and taking Prozac I began to feel some relief. I felt as if heavy weights had been lifted off my chest. This was a very hopeful period for me. I did, however, make a mistake by taking myself off of Prozac thinking I didn't need it anymore. My depression roared back within a couple of weeks."

The best way to ensure the success of your treatment is to follow the suggestions and recommendations of your doctor and/or therapist. This includes sticking with your general treatment plan and following all special instructions.

If you are on antidepressants, following your treatment plan means taking the prescribed dose at the correct time each day. Skipping doses or taking extra pills can harm you and slow your progress. As you begin to feel better you may feel tempted to try going without medication. Don't. Even after the depression lifts you may need to take medications for several more months to prevent an immediate relapse. Never stop a prescribed medication without discussing it first with your doctor.

From time to time, Cognitive Behavioral Therapy (CBT) and Interpersonal Therapy (IPT) therapists give "homework." This usually includes things like writing down your feelings and thoughts that come up between sessions. In the early stages of treatment you may feel too fatigued to do this. The therapist's recommendations are an integral part of the treatment. Making an effort to complete the assignments is essential to recovery.

10. Avoid alcohol and illegal drugs

Alcohol is an addictive substance that can also change and depress mood. Excessive drinking and alcoholism increase the risk of developing Clinical Depression. The same is true for illegal (sometimes called "street") drugs like cocaine, crack, marijuana, and heroin. In addition to risking depression, there is the very real problem of becoming physically dependent on a drug that is prohibited by law.

If you have problems with drinking or using drugs and think that you might have an addiction, speak with your doctor. There are medical programs and community centers that specialize in treating problems with addiction. Alcoholics Anonymous and Narcotics Anonymous are two national organizations that help those with addiction problems. Both organizations have meetings in communities throughout the United States and in most countries.

Table 5.1 and Table 5.2 list some general activities that you can do to help yourself.

Table 5.1 Things I can do to help myself

1. Regular bedtime

2. Daily moderate exercise

3. Decrease stress

4. Avoid being alone for long periods

Table 5.1 Things I can do to help myself (Cont.)

5. Keep scheduled appointments

6. Report any and all medication side effects

7. Eat a healthy diet

8. Avoid taking on new or difficult tasks

9. Follow doctor and therapist recommendations

10. Avoid alcohol and illegal drugs

Table 5.2 Things I can do to help myself

In addition to getting treatment from a professional, there are things that you can do to help yourself. Think about actions or activities that can help your recovery process. Small things can make a big difference, so you don't need to plan special activities or make big changes. List the things that you can do to help yourself.

Pleasant Activities

(List activities that you find enjoyable, fun, rewarding, meaningful, or motivational; e.g., watching a movie, taking a nature walk, reading.)

1.

2.

3.

4.

5.

Relaxing Activities

(Name some activities that help to soothe or relax you and reduce stress and worries; e.g., taking a bath, meditation, spiritual practice.)

6.

7.

8.

9.

10.

Table 5.2 Things I can do to help myself (Cont.)

Exercise, Diet, and Sleep

(What can you do to help yourself maintain a healthy diet, get some regular exercise, and get enough sleep?)

11.

12.

13.

14.

15.

People, Places, Things to Avoid

(Are there things you should stay away from until you are feeling better?)

16.

17.

18.

19.

20.

Other Ideas for Recovery:

21.

22.

23.

24.

25.

CHAPTER 6

COPING WITH
SPECIAL ISSUES

Clinical Depression occurs in people of every race, ethnicity, gender, age, and income. It is a common disorder. Nevertheless, current research reveals that in general medical settings some groups have more difficulty getting the correct diagnosis and appropriate treatment than others. This finding is cause for serious concern. It means that there are segments of our population who must endure the terrible pain and suffering of depression while successful treatments exist.

This chapter looks at some special problems encountered by many with depressive symptoms. In addition to discussing characteristics that put people at additional risk for poor or inadequate care, this section discusses special circumstances that either increase the risk of developing Clinical Depression or significantly change the intensity of care needed to get better.

A. RACE, ETHNICITY, CULTURE

Although there is no credible biological evidence for the concept of race,[1, 2] there are groups that share common cultural characteristics, origins, and experiences. "Ethnicity" is probably a more accurate term than "race" to distinguish social groups. What people usually mean when they talk about race is skin color. It is clear that, for many, skin color plays a powerful role in shaping how others interact with and treat them.

The 2001 United States Surgeon General's Report on Mental Health reported remarkable racial and ethnic group differences in minorities' access to healthcare and in the quality of the healthcare they received.[3] The report states that, "Minorities have less access to, and availability of, mental health services. Minorities are less likely to receive needed mental health services. Minorities in treatment often receive a poorer quality of mental health care."[4] In this report, the phrase "racial and ethnic minority" refers to four main groups: African Americans, Hispanic Americans (including Mexican Americans and others with roots in Spanish-speaking countries), Asian Americans (including Pacific Islanders) and Native Americans (including American Indians and Alaska Natives).

Prejudice, discrimination, cultural misinterpretation, distrust, and poor communication are some of the theories thought to explain why these groups are less likely to receive good quality care. The likely answer is that various combinations of these factors, as well as additional factors such as insurance status, financial status, and community resources determine the type and quality of care a person receives.

Faced with this information, especially if you are a member of an ethnic minority, you may worry that you will have trouble finding the care you need. Although these facts are troubling, they do **not** mean that you cannot find good care. These findings **do** mean that you will need to pay close attention to the way your clinic and clinician treat you.

Dealing with Prejudice and Discrimination

Race, ethnicity, and sexual orientation are three characteristics that can increase the likelihood of encountering prejudice and discrimination. Gender and age are others. If your clinician treats you in a rude, abrupt manner, or appears uninterested, contact the person in charge of the clinic or medical office. You should do the same if the clinician makes inappropriate comments that reveal negative, biased attitudes. The director or chief can arrange to speak with this person and counsel them about the need to treat everyone with respect. This administrator can also arrange for your transfer to the care of another doctor or therapist. An important component of high-quality care is respectful treatment. You do not have to settle for care with someone who disrespects you.

If you live in an area with few doctors or therapists and feel there is no way to transfer your care to someone else, having a frank discussion with the person treating you is one possibility. Prejudice is a highly emotional issue and speaking about it is never easy. There are ways to confront it, however, without getting into heated arguments. Table 6.1 gives sample phrases to use in this situation.

Table 6.1 Suggestions for ways to talk about sensitive issues

"I'm feeling uncomfortable. I'm concerned that my (race, ethnicity, gender, age, sexual orientation) is a problem (or a difficult issue) for you. I'd like to discuss this before going further with my treatment."

"I'm worried that there are misunderstandings or misperceptions about me based on my (ethnicity, gender, age, sexual orientation). I'm also concerned that these things might affect my treatment. Are you open (or willing) to talking about this?"

"Have you worked with many patients of my (ethnicity, gender, age, sexual orientation)? I know that there are misunderstandings or misperceptions surrounding this issue sometimes, so I'd like us to be able to discuss it."

Getting good care is very important. Inadequate or inappropriate treatment jeopardizes your chances for recovery. Bad care can be worse than no care.

B. EXPOSURE TO LIFE-THREATENING EVENTS

Those who go through the ordeal of a life-threatening event almost always experience serious emotional distress. The clinically depressed are especially vulnerable. Even those in treatment can notice that their symptoms increase or worsen, prolonging their recovery.

During the past two hundred years, unprecedented numbers of people experienced catastrophic events. Wars, bombings, massacres, genocide, torture, and terrorism have caused incredible pain and suffering for millions of people. Being a victim of rape, violent crime, a serious accident, or natural disaster, such as a hurricane or earthquake, is also extremely emotionally traumatic. Additionally, terrible events cause emotional trauma for those who witness these events as well as those who escape without physical injury.

The families, friends, and co-workers of those killed, lost, or injured also experience terrible distress. The terrorist attacks of September 11, 2001, killed thousands, but traumatized many thousands more who knew and loved the dead and injured.

Phases of Trauma Recovery[5, 6]

Elisabeth Kübler-Ross was one of the first physicians to document that the process of recovery from trauma occurs in distinct stages.[7] She initially worked with those dying from terminal illness. Clinicians, building on her work, observed that trauma victims go through similar phases of emotional recovery after experiencing a life-threatening event. Those with Clinical Depression go through the same stages after a serious trauma, however, their symptoms are frequently more severe and continue for longer periods of time.

The next section describes the phases of trauma recovery. For the purpose of simplifying the discussion, we divide them into four basic stages: (1) shock and disbelief; (2) anger and sadness; (3) emotional readjustment; and (4) return to usual "before the event" functioning. Emotional symptoms can occur throughout all four phases, but are most intense during the first three. As you'll note, many of the symptoms are similar to those experienced during an episode of Clinical Depression. The difference is that the symptoms begin or, in the case of those with depression, markedly increase, after the major traumatic event.

Phase 1. Shock and Disbelief

The initial emotional response to severe trauma is that of shock and disbelief. Coming so close to dying or witnessing the death and disfigurement of others is more than anyone's mind can grasp right away. Many are frightened and too stunned to talk. Some become panic-stricken and cry uncontrollably.

Sleeplessness, extreme fear, anxiety, recurrent memories of the event, and nightmares are common signs of emotional trauma. Many victims re-experience the horror through vivid flashbacks that occur at unexpected times. Some avoid anything and anyone that reminds them about what happened. Others can't stop thinking or talking about the event.

Symptoms usually begin within hours or days. In some rare instances, however, the signs of emotional trauma appear years after the event.

Typically, the emotional reaction is most severe during the first few weeks and lessens in intensity in the following months. There is no set rule, though. The level of suffering can fluctuate from day to day, with some days or weeks being much worse than others.

Phase 2. Anger and Sadness

Anger and sadness are also part of the recovery. Victims and their loved ones often feel tremendous anger at those who caused the trauma, or, in the case of natural disasters, at nature or at God. Family and friends may become angry with the dead or injured loved one. This is particularly true if they believe that the person, either deliberately or innocently, put himself or herself in harm's way.

Besides anger, victims and their loved ones experience overwhelming sorrow. Tearfulness with frequent crying spells occurs frequently during this time. This second phase is also a time of intense yearning and grieving for life as it was before the event.

In disasters, many survivors have trouble coming to terms with the fact that they lived while others died. The term used to describe this phenomenon is "survivor guilt." As with many of the other symptoms, the feelings of guilt tend to go away as survivors learn to adjust to life after the event.

Phase 3. Emotional Readjustment

During this period, sufferers slowly but steadily find themselves having more good days than bad. There are fewer symptoms and the intensity of feelings is much less severe. Victims begin to come to terms with their life and lifestyle changes brought about by the event.

Phase 4. Return to Normal Functioning

Most people return to normal or near-normal functioning by the end of the first year after the trauma. There is no set timeframe, however. Individuals differ. Some take longer to emotionally regroup. Ongoing trauma, the kind that happens in war, and managing injuries or disabilities that require prolonged medical care, can delay the process of emotional healing.

There are things that can help the recovery process. Early intervention is one. Talking to someone trained in managing emotional trauma is probably best, but support groups made up of other trauma victims also can help. Many emergency-response teams have mental health personnel available to counsel those in need. Trauma hospitals and clinics usually provide emergency mental health staff to assist victims of disasters and violent crime. Several states and community organizations fund victim-assistance programs that pay for counseling and support groups.

The emotional aftermath of any traumatic event can be agonizing. Because of severe emotional pain and anxiety, some victims wonder if their feelings are signs of a serious mental disorder. As you learned in the previous sections, trauma victims can develop symptoms that are similar to those seen in depression. It is also true that these kinds of events can increase the risk of developing a Clinical Depression. "Normal" trauma symptoms differ from Clinical Depression in two fundamental ways: (1) symptoms related to the trauma start almost immediately after experiencing or witnessing a life-threatening event and, (2) over time, these symptoms show sometimes slow but consistent improvement. In Clinical Depression, symptoms don't usually improve, in fact, they tend to get worse over time. This is a major warning sign. If this happens to you, even after a serious traumatic event, see a doctor.

C. CHILD AND ADOLESCENT DEPRESSION[8]

"Please let parents know that if their child shows strange behavior, not to count it off as typical childhood problems. Growing up problems. Some signs I had that were not taken seriously were: a loner, very quiet, does not participate in class, always taking blame, too passive. These are a few signs

*I know I put out. No one recognized that they could be a problem. This is
not a problem for everyone, but it is better to be safe than sorry. I was one
of the lucky ones. Some children are not so lucky."*

Adults are not the only ones who become clinically depressed.
Children and adolescents can also suffer with this very disabling
disorder. Childhood depression is very similar to adult depression;
however, depending on a child's age and stage of emotional development, the onset may be more subtle and the symptoms somewhat
different.

Most young children have trouble expressing their feelings in
words. Adolescents, too, often struggle when trying to express how
they feel. Behavior is the primary way most children and adolescents express emotional distress. For this reason, any significant
change in behavior, especially an increase in negative or "acting-
out" behavior, should raise warning flags about the child's or adolescent's emotional state. In childhood depression, negative or
destructive behaviors occur throughout the day, almost every day,
and last for weeks.

Ongoing agitation, with hyperactivity, restlessness, and acting
out are common symptoms of childhood depression. The same is
true for continual problems with irritability, grouchiness, and anger.
Many of the symptoms overlap with those seen in Attention Deficit
and Hyperactivity Disorders. What distinguishes depression from
these other disorders is the fact that these symptoms represent a
change from the child's or teenager's previous ways of behaving.

Like others with depression, children can become emotionally
withdrawn and refuse to participate in family activities and social
events. Friendships suffer as they lose interest in their friends. Even
very young children can lose interest in play and other activities
that they enjoyed in the past.

Frequent complaints of stomachaches, headaches, and other body aches and pains are especially common in young children with depression. Sleep and appetite problems can also occur, but are less likely in this age group.

Deterioration in school performance is one of the first signs of depression in school-age children and adolescents. Their grades drop as they struggle to focus and pay attention in class. Many lose interest in schoolwork and stop participating in extracurricular activities. Some children thought to have learning disabilities actually have Clinical Depression. In these cases, the learning disability resolves when the child recovers.

Teenage depression looks more like adult depression, although adolescents typically don't complain of problems with sleep and appetite. Substance abuse can become a major problem when they use alcohol and illegal drugs to relieve their emotional pain. Figure 6.1 shows the cycle of symptoms for depressed adolescents and children.

As with adults, children can get caught in a downward spiral of escalating problems at home and at school. Children with the most severe forms of depression feel hopeless. Some become preoccupied with death and consider suicide. The second leading cause of death for teenagers is suicide. Adolescent males, particularly African Americans, Hispanic Americans, and Native Americans, are especially vulnerable. The suicide rate for ethnic-minority-group boys is higher than the national average. Adolescent girls also try to kill themselves, but their rate of completed suicide is much lower. Suicide in young children is rare. Section E discusses suicide in more detail.

Finding good care for children and adolescents often requires a great deal of effort on the part of parents and guardians. Children are not "little adults." Their emotional and biological needs are dif-

Figure 6.1 Child and adolescent depression: the cycle of symptoms

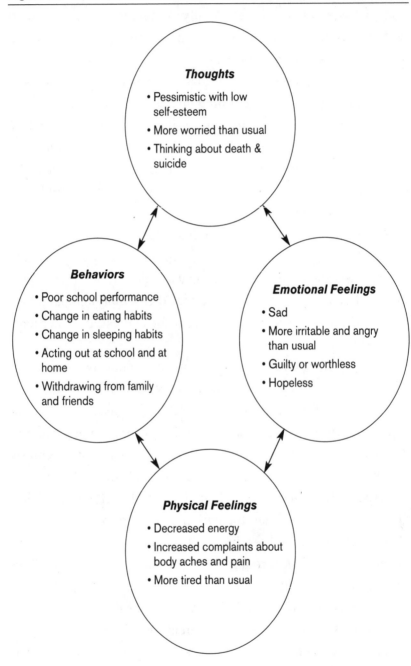

Thoughts
- Pessimistic with low self-esteem
- More worried than usual
- Thinking about death & suicide

Behaviors
- Poor school performance
- Change in eating habits
- Change in sleeping habits
- Acting out at school and at home
- Withdrawing from family and friends

Emotional Feelings
- Sad
- More irritable and angry than usual
- Guilty or worthless
- Hopeless

Physical Feelings
- Decreased energy
- Increased complaints about body aches and pain
- More tired than usual

ferent. Because of this, their care is more complex. They require special forms of psychotherapy and individually tailored doses of antidepressant medication when indicated.

If, after reading this section, you suspect that your child suffers from Clinical Depression, it is vitally important that you get them assessed by a qualified clinician, someone experienced in identifying and treating childhood emotional problems. The first step is discussing the situation with your child's doctor. If your pediatrician or family doctor has little or no experience in diagnosing and treating childhood depression, ask for a referral to a psychologist (Ph.D.) or psychiatrist (M.D.) who specializes in child and adolescent disorders.

As with adults, the severity of the Clinical Depression determines the type of treatment recommended.

D. DEPRESSION IN THE ELDERLY

"Living by myself; taking care of my home and yard, and being a senior citizen on a small monthly income have been factors in my having down periods."

Clinical Depression is common among the elderly. The risk increases with age and is highest after age 80. This finding appears to relate to the fact that a large number of older adults have several of the same factors that increase depression risk in other groups. For example, seniors are more likely to experience many losses, including the death of a spouse or loved one. Many struggle to live on fixed incomes and fall into poverty. Social isolation is common. The elderly are also more likely to have serious and disabling medical conditions.

The symptoms of depression are the same for the elderly as for younger adults. As with children and adolescents, the onset of symptoms in older adults is frequently subtle. One of the major problems is that the medical disorders combined with the medications that the elderly often take can mask the beginning stages of a depression.

Many assume that the slowed thinking, poor memory, and problems with concentration that accompany depression are signs of worsening medical illness. Some worry about senility or diseases like Alzheimer's.

Complaints of fatigue, body aches and pains, and problems with sleep are common in syndromes like heart disease, diabetes, and arthritis. These and similar symptoms are also common in neurological diseases like Parkinson's and multiple sclerosis.

Diagnosing Clinical Depression is especially difficult when the elderly suffer from several forms of illness that have clinical symptoms overlapping or the same as those seen in depression. Furthermore, to complicate matters, some of the medications that effectively treat medical problems common in the elderly also increase the risk of developing depression (see Chapter 2 and The Appendix). Seniors who don't have medical illnesses can also overlook early symptoms. They mistakenly believe that their lack of energy is simply a sign of getting old. They think that their growing feelings of sadness come from having to cope with the many losses and changes that occur with aging.

Some of the barriers to getting care are more significant for the elderly, particularly when they are poor and live alone. Although most seniors have Medicare, many do not have the kind of supplemental insurance that covers extensive psychological care or antidepressant medication. Those who don't drive and live in areas without good public transportation can have problems getting to the doctor's office. Those who need the assistance of a family member or caretaker can face similar problems.

Fortunately, most states and counties have social service agencies that specialize in care for the aged. Many areas have senior centers and other institutions prepared to help the elderly. Any one of these organizations can be a good source for information about transportation and other assistance. Chapter 4 reviews other barriers and gives suggestions on how to overcome them.

A thorough medical evaluation is as important for an elderly person as for others experiencing depressive symptoms. Because, as a group, they have more medical conditions and take more medications, they need a good assessment of their health status before starting any treatment.

Medication side effects are more common, and often more serious in the elderly. Those taking several prescriptions confront the risk of potentially dangerous drug interactions. For these reasons, seniors with serious medical illness who have mild to moderate depressive symptoms may want to avoid medications. ECT is an option for those with severe Clinical Depression. All of these are issues to discuss with the doctor performing the clinical evaluation. Elders with severe depression may be referred to a geriatric psychiatrist, a physician who specializes in the diagnosis and treatment of emotional disorders in people age 65 and older.

Fortunately, most older adults respond to treatment in the same way as their younger counterparts. Good treatment works to help seniors recover from Clinical Depression. Although serious medical problems may narrow the treatment options, they do not prevent someone from recovering from this mood disorder. Getting good care is as successful, and, therefore, as important, for the elderly as it is for other adults and children.

One of the critical problems for older adults with depression is having constant or increasing thoughts about death and dying. Those with severe depression may begin to long for death and seriously consider suicide. Older men carry one of the highest risks of killing themselves. Learning when to get help is crucial. The next section discusses suicide and talks about ways to recognize when it's time to get emergency help.

E. PERSISTENT THOUGHTS OF DEATH AND SUICIDE

"It was so frustrating. I got to the point where I wanted to be put away. I even tried committing suicide. I know now that is not the solution, but the end. Nothing would have been settled."

The most serious symptom for anyone with depression is suicidal thoughts. Sufferers begin to feel that there is no way to get relief, that there is no way out of the intense emotional pain. They lose hope and begin to think that death is the only way to stop the pain. Although not everyone who thinks about death seriously considers suicide, it is a dangerous symptom. The risk of suicide, especially for those with depression, is real.

While both men and women attempt suicide, men are more likely to kill themselves. Teenage boys have a higher rate of suicide than teenage girls. The risk for men increases with age and is highest for men over age 65. Males are more likely to use a gun or other methods with a high fatality rate. Women are more likely to take an overdose of pills.

Research looking at suicidal behavior reveals that there are several factors that can increase the risk of making an attempt.[9] Briefly, they are: age (older than 45); being male; alcohol and drug abuse; previous suicide attempts; Clinical Depression; long duration of the depression; recent losses; declining physical health; not working; and being single (including widowed, legally separated, and divorced). It is important to note that risk factors are not absolute predictors of who will commit suicide. Those without any risk factors can make an attempt.

Not everyone with suicidal thoughts attempts suicide. Some who think about death and dying do not seriously consider killing themselves. Religious faith or worry about the effect of their death on loved ones prevents many from ever making an attempt.

"When times got hard, I many a time wanted to leave this world. It was the love I had for my three children and, yes, the scare of losing them, if I actually went through with suicide [that stopped me]."

The two most important questions to ask someone who is talking about wanting to die are "Are you thinking about how you would do it?" and "Have you thought about when you'd do it?" An answer to "how?" can indicate that a person is imagining or planning a specific way to die. An answer to "when" is of even more concern. It means that the person is close to attempting suicide. Formulating a plan is one of the most important predictors of a suicide attempt.

Suicidal thoughts are always a **very** serious matter. They can occur in all forms of depression and at any level of severity. Members of all ages and ethnic groups can begin to think seriously about killing themselves.

Remember, depression affects the way you think about yourself and the world. Feeling pessimistic and hopeless is part of the illness. For those already in care, suicidal thoughts may indicate that the treatment plan needs to be re-evaluated. For those who are not in treatment, suicidal thoughts indicate the need for careful medical assessment.

If you or your loved one begin to think about death and to fantasize about ways to die, let your doctor know right away. You need an immediate assessment to see if it is safe for you to stay at home.

F. PREGNANCY

If you are trying to get pregnant, or are pregnant, tell your doctor right away. Pregnancy can affect your treatment options. The potential adverse effects of medications are always a concern for pregnant women or those who are trying to get pregnant. Although there is some early evidence that antidepressant medications are safe during pregnancy, the true risks are not known.

Women of childbearing age, and those trying to get pregnant, should be especially careful when considering medications for an episode of Clinical Depression. There is evidence that medications other than antidepressants—tranquilizers, sedatives, and other mood stabilizers—can have potentially dangerous effects on the mother and/or the unborn child, especially during the early months of pregnancy. This does not mean that pregnant women cannot take any of these medications. Before taking any pills (prescribed or not) they should carefully discuss and review all medicines with their doctor and/or OB-GYN specialist. Those with diagnosed depression should discuss medication choices with their doctor before trying to get pregnant. For women with mild to moderate symptoms, psychotherapy, especially one of the effective forms discussed earlier in this book (Cognitive Behavioral Therapy or Interpersonal Therapy) may be an effective choice for treatment. If a pregnant woman's depression is very severe and if she becomes suicidal, however, there may be no choice but to consider medication and/or hospitalization.

All of the special issues presented in this chapter represent areas of particular concern. Reviewing each topic can help you anticipate problems and give you a strategy for finding a solution.

CHAPTER 7

LIVING WITH DEPRESSION

Those with Clinical Depression already understand that living with depression is no easy feat. It takes a great deal of courage to begin each day knowing that even simple things like getting out of bed, require monumental effort. Yet there are millions who summon the strength to struggle through, hoping that somehow, some way, things will get better.

As we discussed in previous chapters, with treatment, there is good reason to hope. Recovery is the rule, *not* the exception. Without treatment, symptoms of Clinical Depression almost always become more severe. Depressed people who don't get care can find themselves caught in a maze of worsening symptoms, feeling that there is no way out. While some people—the minority—get better on their own, there's no way to tell if that will happen to you. Waiting to find out if you'll get better on your own may take months, even years. Almost everyone needs good treatment to recover.

Even with good treatment, life doesn't immediately return to normal. Recovery takes time. There are many paths to recovery, and sometimes you have to switch or add new treatments for a good result.

This chapter is about the steady, but sometimes slow, process of healing. The first section gives an overview of the important things to know about the process of recovery. We explain the four stages of recovery and review ways to recognize when your treatment plan is not working and needs adjusting.

The second section covers home and job issues. It discusses important topics like confidentiality that can impact your family and work life. Privacy is a central concern for those who fear misunderstanding or mistreatment if they reveal that they suffer with Clinical Depression.

The third, and final, section of this chapter discusses ways to recognize a later episode of Clinical Depression. The clinical term for this is *relapse*. Despite everyone's best efforts, there are times when depressive symptoms return. This is not a sign of failure of either the initial treatment or you. Depression is simply an illness that sometimes recurs. A relapse can happen after months, or years, of feeling fine. Fortunately, relapses respond to treatment as well as first episodes. They are less likely to happen if you recover fully from any earlier episodes. Early treatment is as important for any recurrence or relapse as it is for the first episode. Delayed care results in prolonged and needless pain.

STAGES OF RECOVERY FROM CLINICAL DEPRESSION

"I had a dedicated therapist and she helped me get to the point of realizing my life had to change."

One of the most difficult things about the period between starting treatment and feeling better is that it requires a great deal of patience at a time when sufferers want relief to come quickly. As is true for other serious medical illnesses, treatments don't improve depressive symptoms overnight. Psychotherapy and antidepressants are not like antibiotics that eliminate symptoms within hours and cure disease within days. In Clinical Depression, most people start feeling better within the first few weeks, but it can be more than a month before they notice significant improvement. The time to full recovery, to living completely free of symptoms, can take longer. The healing occurs in phases over several months.

The process of recovery typically occurs in four stages: Initiation of treatment, Response, Remission, and Recovery.[1] The time spent in each phase is highly variable, because it depends on the severity of symptoms and the quality of the response to therapy and/or medication.

Learning about these stages can help you gauge your progress. You can monitor your improvement by keeping a weekly record of any current symptoms. Make several photocopies of the symptom checklist provided in the Appendix or use a journal to document how you're feeling.

In early phases of treatment, it's a good idea to monitor your symptoms each week. After the first month, you can record them every 2 weeks. After several months, you can switch to tracking your symptoms monthly or so. You may need to keep tracking for six to twelve months to make sure that you are consistently improving and staying well.

Stage 1—Initiation of Treatment

"When my counselor wanted me to go on medication—That is when I decided that I would snap out of this hell I was living...."

The first stage of recovery, the acute phase, begins the day you start your treatment regimen. If you choose psychotherapy, it starts with your first session. If you take medication, it starts with your first dose. With ECT, it begins with your first procedure.

The time from starting treatment to noticing partial improvement can take a few weeks. Some people notice some improvement within two weeks; however, most find that it takes up to a month before they begin to feel significantly better. Physical symptoms like sleep, appetite, and fatigue are generally among the first to improve. The sadness and pessimism take longer to resolve.

This stage lasts about the same amount of time that it takes the human body to mend a broken bone. An uncomplicated fracture heals in about six weeks. The first phase also takes about six weeks, but can last up to twelve weeks. This analogy also applies to the general way depression treatments work. A cast stabilizes and protects an injured bone, thus allowing it to heal. Psychotherapy and medications function in a similar way. They both "stabilize" depression and initiate the healing process.

For those in psychotherapy, this is the period of learning new techniques for coping with the situations and relationships that impact your symptoms. It is a period for learning not only about what hurts, but also what helps you. Doing the homework assignments and applying your therapist's suggestions are essential. Not doing these things can jeopardize your chances for improvement.

For those receiving medication, this is the time when your doctor and you will decide which medication(s) and which dose(s) to use. The initial dosing regimen is not always the one that you stay with. Depending on your sensitivity to the initial medication and side effects, your doctor may need to make minor or major adjustments to your regimen. The physician may take antidepressant blood levels to determine the appropriate dose for you. This is the period of time when all of these issues get worked out.

Towards the end of this phase, the severity of the depression should begin to diminish. Although many of the depressive symptoms are still present, most are much less intense. Because depressive symptoms resolve slowly, the person with the depression is often the last to recognize that they are gradually getting better. Family and friends are typically the first to comment on the gradual lifting of spirits. Each week should bring added relief. *If, by the end of the first 6 weeks, you feel no improvement or you feel worse, your doctor or therapist needs to reassess and change the regimen or refer you to a specialist.*

For all patients with any illness, it can be difficult to follow treatments "just as the doctor ordered." It's common for people on antibiotics to feel tempted to stop when they feel well. Just as with antibiotics, though, stopping antidepressants in the middle of treatment can lead to a relapse or return of the problem.

Stage 2—Response to Treatment

"What would [I] recommend to others in [my] situation? First, not to be afraid to ask for help. Second, to listen to yourself. If you know things are not right, get help. Third, don't give up. It will not go away overnight. Learn the signs and how to deal with it. It could be a lifelong fight. However, with help from [our doctors], it can be a lot easier to get through it. I still have down times, but nothing like before. Life is wonderful."

The second stage of recovery begins when the treatment regimen stabilizes. Psychotherapy and/or medication routines are settled and no longer need significant restructuring. There is noticeable improvement in almost all of the depressive symptoms. Remaining symptoms are much milder than at the start of treatment.

Hobbies and social activities become interesting again. Pessimism decreases. Work at home and on the job is easier and takes a lot less effort. Some still experience occasional "blue" days, but bounce back quickly. Periods of feeling downhearted or discouraged don't last for days or weeks on end. The shadow of depression fades.

Using a checklist to keep a record of the gradual decline in the severity and number of symptoms is helpful during this period. This gives tangible evidence that the Clinical Depression is responding to treatment.

People feel tremendous relief when they reach this stage. Because of this, some give in to the temptation to take on new or difficult projects. They wrongly assume that feeling better indicates that everything is back to normal. This is a serious mistake. The added stress of additional work can cause a serious setback. The analogy of the broken leg applies here, too. Taking on a new or challenging task before the depression thoroughly resolves is like jogging before the fracture completely heals. Those who do this risk re-injury. There is the real danger of prolonging their illness. Following the doctor and therapist's recommendations is as important during this phase as in the beginning of treatment.

The amount of time spent in this stage depends on how long it takes for symptoms to resolve. Usually by the third month of consistent treatment, most symptoms show marked improvement. By the end of this stage, few, if any, symptoms are still present.

Stage 3—Remission of Symptoms

"After a couple months of weekly therapy and taking [medication], I began to feel some relief. I felt as if heavy weights had been lifted off my chest."

During this stage, most, if not all, depressive symptoms diminish or disappear. This stage is also called the Maintenance phase of recovery. It refers to the fact that depressed people still need some form of treatment to maintain their improvement. By this point, those with Clinical Depression no longer look depressed. They function at near-normal levels.

Physical aches and pains caused by, or associated with, depression decrease. The ability to concentrate and focus on details returns to normal. Those who previously enjoyed reading look forward to starting a new book. The same is true for hobbies and other leisure activities.

Those who participated in Cognitive or Interpersonal Psychotherapy need to continue practicing the skills learned in therapy. People who consistently apply these techniques and principles usually note steady improvement.

Those on medication need to continue taking antidepressants as prescribed and keep follow-up appointments with their doctor. The temptation to discontinue medication is greatest during this period, because people feel so much better. Those with lingering side effects may want to decrease or stop taking their medications. Doing so is dangerous and significantly increases the chances that symptoms will not only return, but get much worse. Routine follow-up, while continuing to take medication, is vital to sustaining and enhancing recovery.

Most people should continue taking their antidepressant medication a few months after getting completely well to make sure that the episode has fully healed.

"I work every day to keep going, taking one day at a time. I even tried to go off my depression medication a couple times, saying, 'Oh, I can do it on my own.' That's a joke."

Stage 4—Recovery and Termination of Treatment

This stage starts after a prolonged period of treatment without perceptible signs of Clinical Depression. The typical amount of time is between four and nine months. During this time, people are essentially symptom-free and able to handle work and family life without much difficulty. This doesn't mean that everything in life is perfect. People still experience the normal ups and downs of daily living. Still, at this point, they can manage without becoming overwhelmed. This is the time to consider discontinuing treatment.

Some medications require a gradual taper. Stopping them too abruptly can cause uncomfortable side effects. For example, insomnia, physical aches, nausea, and anxiety are some side effects that occur when tricyclic antidepressants aren't carefully tapered. These side effects don't normally last for more than a week or two, but they cause unnecessary discomfort. The tapering process for antidepressant medication can take anywhere from two to eight weeks, depending on the type of medication and the individual's response to stopping.

This stage is also the time for those in therapy to review their readiness to end psychotherapy. There may be other personal issues that require additional help and insight. Those living in difficult circumstances may need the additional emotional support that psychotherapy provides. Others may be ready to stop.

After months of feeling well, some are afraid that symptoms will return and their lives will deteriorate if they stop any of their treatments. Family members may add to these fears and concerns by questioning the wisdom of going off treatment; others may urge them to stop treatment before they are ready. For those who experience anxiety about bringing treatment to a close, discussing the situation with their treating clinician can help. There are several options that can ease the termination process.

The first alternative is to continue treatment for another three to six months before making a decision. During this time, psychotherapy sessions, medication doses, and medical visits can continue as usual.

The second option is to start a very slow taper, spacing out therapy sessions and/or decreasing medication over the course of months rather than weeks.

The third alternative is to arrange a two-to-three month trial without treatment. (This plan is not advised for persons with a history of multiple depressions or risk factors for relapse.) This arrangement should include a specific date to review and reassess the need for further care. The success of the trial depends on contacting the doctor or therapist right away when troubling symptoms begin. Waiting until the next scheduled appointment wouldn't be wise and might increase the risk of the depression returning.

Full recovery signals the end of the Clinical Depression. People begin to live normal lives again. In some cases, particularly for those who gained insight from psychotherapy, their lives improve.

THE RETURN OF SYMPTOMS DURING TREATMENT

There are times when depressive symptoms resurface during treatment. Between 10 and 20% of people have this experience.[2] It can happen at any stage of the recovery process. For most, these episodes last for a short while and are not very severe. They are usually mild and go away without any need for clinical intervention. If symptoms continue, worsen or become severe, however, the treatment plan needs review. Continuing symptoms indicate that there is an inadequate or poor response to the current regimen.

Recovery is the rule and not the exception; nonetheless, there are instances when people need ongoing, long-term, treatment. For a small number of people, troubling symptoms return whenever they try to terminate treatment. They need to continue treatment for much longer periods.

More rare than the return of depressive symptoms during treatment is the development of a syndrome called "mania" after starting an antidepressant medication. "Mania" is a rapid acceleration of mood to the point where people feel agitated, nervous, or irritable. They speak quickly and ideas race through their head. They sleep less, but don't feel tired. These symptoms indicate the presence of an underlying illness called Manic Depression or Bipolar Disorder. There are successful treatments for Bipolar Disorder, but they are different than the medications used to treat Clinical Depression. We reviewed this disorder in Chapter 3. If manic symptoms emerge during treatment for depression, your doctor should refer you to a psychiatrist.

If there is a history of Bipolar Disorder in your family, you should alert your doctor during the initial phase of choosing a treatment. Even though a positive family history of manic-depressive illness increases the risk of this illness, not everyone with family history develops manic symptoms when they take antidepressants. Your doctor will want to monitor your symptoms very closely, however.

WORK AND FAMILY ISSUES

Many people with Clinical Depression have concerns about disclosing their feelings and experiences to loved ones and people at work. They don't know how to talk about their depression and worry that others will respond negatively. Some worry that others will look at them differently, seeing them as permanently impaired or mentally unfit.

Another worry is that private medical information will leak out and expose them to bad consequences at work, or hurt their chances for future employment. Many fear that their boss or supervisor will react by giving them a bad evaluation, reducing their rank, or even firing them.

This section focuses on work and family issues for those recovering from Clinical Depression. It discusses ways to minimize or overcome the fears associated with disclosing such personal information.

Privacy Issues at Work

There are federal laws that govern the disclosure of medical information. For the most part, you have the ability to determine who gets information about your illness and clinical care. If your job provides your health insurance, however, there is a real possibility that someone in your Human Resources department knows when you receive treatment for depression.

To process your claims, your health insurance requires documentation of the diagnosis that prompted treatment. They also have access to your medical records as part of their review process. If this concerns you, you need to talk with your treating clinician about the level of detail used in your medical record.

Some high-risk and high-level security jobs restrict the kinds of medications that employees can take while working. This situation may require workers to take an extended leave or transfer to a lower-level job during the recovery period. Fortunately, most people with Clinical Depression need treatment for a relatively short period of time and can return to a full level of work.

The major concern for most people with depression is whether to tell the manager or boss about the illness and, if so, when and what to disclose. One of the key determinants is how you function at work. This includes your ability to get to work, stay at work, and complete the tasks assigned to you.

Those with mild depression can often continue to work, although they may struggle to keep a normal pace. They may determine that telling their boss is unnecessary, because their work performance is at a high enough level that they can manage while the treatment takes effect. Taking on especially difficult assignments may cause problems in their recovery, however. The wise course of action may be to talk with the boss.

Those with moderate depression may work, but frequently find themselves falling behind or missing deadlines. At this point, the supervisor and colleagues probably notice that something is wrong. Alerting the boss to the fact that you have a medical problem and are in treatment can help make adjustments in your workload until you are back to normal.

Those with severe depression are usually so impaired that they can't complete assignments and use more sick days than other employees. Those who do not disclose something about the true reason for their low functioning risk getting poor evaluations and jeopardizing their future in that job. Those with moderate to severe depression will probably want to negotiate for a reduced workload until they are well enough to take on more assignments.

Talking with a boss or supervisor is not easy. Telling him or her that you have a medical disorder and are in treatment may be all that is necessary. Depending on the kind of relationship that you have with your boss, you may not need to state the exact nature of your illness. If you trust your boss to help you while keeping your information private, you may decide to disclose that you suffer with Clinical Depression. You can share this book to help him or her learn about this disorder.

Most supervisors will ask for some form of documentation, especially to justify a workload or schedule change. The treating doctor can write a simple note documenting that there is a medical illness and stating that you are in treatment. If asked about the expected recuperation time, you can give an estimate based on your current stage of recovery. As reviewed earlier in this chapter, the average time from starting treatment to significant response is from 6 to 12 weeks.

In the most extreme cases, sufferers need to request temporary medical disability while they recover from depression. Medical doctors must certify the disability and complete the necessary forms.

Most states supply some form of medical compensation for disabled workers, but lengths of time and amounts of money vary. Some states have laws that protect those needing temporary medical disability. Checking with the Human Resources or Personnel Department is a good way to find out about your rights with respect to returning to your same job and workplace after full recovery.

Caution: If you must leave your job, check on the possibility of continuing your present insurance policy so that you remain insured.

Talking with work colleagues is a very personal and individual decision. If your job requires you to collaborate with others to complete assignments, informing them that you have a medical disorder, but expect to fully recover, may help keep their goodwill. Instead of informing them yourself, you may want to ask your supervisor to quietly inform those who need to know.

Talking with Family and Friends

"To me it meant I was less than a man at times when I thought of not being able to help around the home with physical tasks and duties. . . . [Treatment] was a big help to me in helping me talk about my problems and worries. It helped me open up more to my family and I was able to recognize that they were there to support me for as long as it took to get back to helping them."

You have a right to your privacy, even with family and friends. You must weigh your discomfort with disclosure against your real need for their help. Those who live with you on a day-to-day basis are probably already aware that something is seriously wrong. In fact, they may have a better sense of your mood and level of impairment than you, in the beginning. People close to you are also affected by this illness.

Spouses or relationship partners go through experiences that are almost as intense as the person with the depression. They, too, suffer when they watch their loved one go through this kind of anguish. In the early phases of treatment, they need to take on major responsibilities such as keeping track of appointments, remembering the names of medications and doses, keeping records of symptoms, and participating in discussions with the doctor about preferences for treatment.

Even so, talking with loved ones is not easy when you feel so unhappy or when you worry about bothering them with your fears. If you feel that you can't discuss your depression with your partner, ask your doctor or therapist to help you explain. They can meet with both of you and go over any concerns.

If you aren't married or in an intimate relationship, talking with sympathetic relatives and friends can help you weather the sometimes long process of finding a clinician, getting the diagnosis, and starting treatment. People with moderate to severe symptoms need assistance until they reach the point where symptoms no longer interfere with their lives. Sharing concerns with loved ones can help them learn how to provide the support you need.

Talking with children is also important. Children are very sensitive to their parents' moods. They may not understand the exact nature of the problem, but they do know that something is not right. Children often assume that a parent's change in behavior is their fault. This holds true regardless of whether the parent is irritable, sad, or withdrawn. They need reassurance that they are not the cause of their parent's pain.

The decision about what to tell children depends on their age and level of emotional maturity. Very young children don't need long or detailed explanations. They won't grasp the concept of this kind of medical illness and will probably become confused. They do understand that people have days when they have pain or don't feel well. They also know that people sometimes need to take medicine and go to the doctor. Using plain words and simple explanations is best. Here is an example of one way to talk to a young child:

"Mommy [or Daddy] isn't feeling well right now. I need a doctor's help to get better. I'm not sad because of you. You didn't do anything wrong. Things are going to get better, but it may take a little time. Just remember that I love you very much."

Older children and adolescents can understand more complex concepts. Through television, books, or their own experiences they have more familiarity with illness. Telling them about depression, and giving them accurate information, can keep them from becoming confused. Teenagers who want to know more can read sections of this book. Emphasizing the real hope of complete recovery helps allay their fears. Children of all ages need reassurance.

It is important to continue talking and interacting with children, whatever their age. Many children feel a sense of rejection when a parent becomes depressed and emotionally withdrawn. Excluding them can make them feel unwanted or unloved.

When children and adolescents feel worried or upset, they are much more likely to behave in ways that get them into trouble at home and at school. This is a normal way for them to communicate distress. This is an added burden for a mother or father with Clinical Depression, however, especially when they shoulder parenting responsibilities by themselves. When depressed parents feel overwhelmed by their child's response to their illness, they may need to have a family session with a counselor or therapist. Those not already in therapy can ask their doctor for a referral to a counselor. The therapist or counselor can also give suggestions about whether and how to include children without burdening them.

Sometimes when a parent becomes depressed, a child becomes depressed, too. When children become depressed, a depressed parent may miss it. If you feel you are barely hanging on yourself as you try to recover, then recruit a family member or trusted friend to help you with making sure your child receives an evaluation and any needed treatment.

RECOGNIZING A RECURRENCE OR RELAPSE

"In that depression, [in my case], is chronic, I've done well. Occasionally I still experience terrible days, but I've learned a thing or two about coping and am able to persevere. [I cope] by trying to organize my thinking so that I can recognize the onset of an episode and act accordingly."

Sometimes, after years without symptoms, a person will experience a second episode of Clinical Depression. About half of the people with Clinical Depression go on to develop a second or third episode later in life. Unfortunately, the chance of experiencing another depression increases with each new episode. Ninety percent of people with a history of three episodes go on to have a fourth.[3] Again, the good news is that the effectiveness of treatments doesn't diminish. Often the same medication, or class of medications, used to successfully treat the first episode is equally effective for later occurrences of the disorder. Again, recovery is the rule and not the exception.

Recognizing a relapse is important, because getting help early can keep the depression from becoming severe. The signs and symptoms of a recurrence are the same as for the initial episode. Problems with sleep, appetite, energy level, and mood return. Symptoms can have a slow or fast onset. It depends on the individual. The same risk factors and circumstances apply to later episodes. Financial, physical, and emotional setbacks can set the stage for a relapse.

When a relapse occurs, the major consideration is how long to treat the depression. There are special circumstances that can indicate the need for long-term treatment with antidepressant medication. When this happens, ongoing treatment can last for a period of a few years to several decades. The length of treatment depends on the severity and frequency of previous depressions. Clinicians consider long-term maintenance treatment for those with three or more episodes of Clinical Depression. They also consider continuous treatment for patients experiencing at least two depressive episodes with the following conditions: 1) two episodes within a five-year period, 2) strong family history of recurrent mood disorders, 3) first episode of depression before 20 years old, 4) two severe episodes with serious thoughts about suicide, and 5) a relapse within twelve months of stopping a successful medication regimen.[4]

People who have both chronic depression (Dysthymic Disorder) and Major Depression are more likely to need longer-term treatment. If you fall into any of these categories, you and your doctor should consider long-term medication maintenance. The primary goal of continuous treatment is to prevent a recurrence of Clinical Depression.

Table 7.1 gives you a list to check for warning signs of a relapse.

Table 7.1 Warning signs: Am I becoming depressed again?*

Put a checkmark by the symptoms you experienced before getting treatment. Review this list from time to time to help you notice if you are becoming clinically depressed again.

✔	Symptom	How I feel now. Is it time to seek help again?
	Feeling sad or "empty"	
	Loss of interest in things that used to be enjoyable, like sex, sports, reading, or listening to music	
	Trouble concentrating, thinking, remembering, or making decisions	
	Trouble sleeping or sleeping too much	
	Loss of energy or feeling tired	
	Loss of appetite or eating too much	
	Losing weight or gaining weight without trying	
	Crying or feeling like crying a lot	
	Feeling irritable or "on edge"	
	Feeling worthless or guilty	
	Feeling hopeless or negative	
	Thinking a lot about death, including thoughts about suicide	
	Frequent headaches, body aches, and pains	
	Stomach and digestive trouble with bowel irregularity	
	Other symptoms:	

* If you start experiencing these symptoms again, talk to your doctor.

CHAPTER 8

PUTTING IT ALL TOGETHER: STAYING WELL

In depression, recovery is a process and not a single, isolated event. Even in the best of circumstances, healing is a gradual, sometimes slow return to feeling normal. The whole process requires a great deal of patience. Because sufferers and their loved ones are so relieved when the depression lifts, they sometimes forget to think about ways to stay well. They don't realize that after the symptoms improve, they need to shift their attention to maintaining health, to doing the things that can protect against a relapse. Staying well is as important as getting well.

The first part of this chapter briefly recaps and reviews important topics covered by previous chapters. It gives an overview of key issues to consider while going through the process of getting care *and* getting well. Chapter 8 is very similar to a travel guide that highlights major areas and warns you about potential obstacles. In this case, the guide walks travelers through the process of recognizing and getting treatment for a depressive episode. In other words, the journey begins with the recognition of depressive symptoms and ends with entry into recovery.

The second part of the chapter focuses on staying well. It explores ways to prepare for life after a depressive episode resolves. This section takes all of the topics presented in previous chapters and synthesizes them into a simple self-management plan for staying well. A plan does not guarantee that you will never experience another depressive episode, but it helps you anticipate problems and develop a strategy for dealing with them. A plan of action is like a fire drill. You hope to never experience a fire, but in the event that you do, you're prepared.

PART I. SUMMARIZING THE JOURNEY

This section recaps the journey from depression to recovery. Like any good travel guide, this chapter provides a map. The map is in the form of a diagram that outlines seven major questions and nine crucial steps. It is important to answer each question fully before proceeding because your answers are crucial and determine the next step. Figure 8.1 presents a simple diagram of the questions and steps to use as you plan.

Question 1. Do I have depressive symptoms?

This is the first and most basic question, and it is very complex. It's difficult, if not impossible, to find a person who would deny ever having had a period when they felt downhearted or "blue." Almost everyone has occasional periods when they feel sad or out-of-sorts. Nevertheless, Clinical Depression is a common disorder, one that affects women and men of all ages, races, and incomes. If you have depressive symptoms, you *might* have Clinical Depression.

Step 1. Learn the common symptoms

Chapter 1 reviewed common depressive symptoms and highlighted the important differences between the blues and more serious illness.

Figure 8.1 Steps from depression to recovery

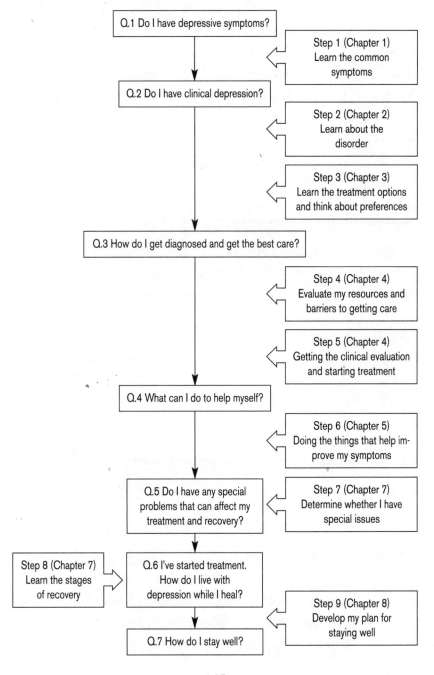

The blues come and go. They seldom linger for weeks or months without some periods of relief. In Clinical Depression, people experience symptoms most of the day, almost every day for weeks, months and sometimes years. The blues make people feel awful, but they rarely interfere with their ability to function. People with Clinical Depression struggle to manage the activities of daily life.

Step 2. Learn more about the disorder

The major point of the second chapter is that Clinical Depression is a medical disorder, a clinical illness that affects the mood. It is not just one disorder, however; there are many different types of Clinical Depression. The various types differ in the number of symptoms, the intensity of symptoms, and how long symptoms last.

Chapter 2 also talked about the circumstances and personal situations that can increase the risk of having a depressive episode.

Question 2. Do I have Clinical Depression?

After learning the symptoms and reading more about the illness, you may realize that the chances are good that you have Clinical Depression. Again, the good news is that Clinical Depression is a treatable illness. Depending on the number and severity of symptoms, there are a number of treatment options. While considering all of this, it helps to remember that recovery is the rule, and not the exception.

Step 3. Learn the treatment options and begin to think about preferences

Chapter 3 reviewed the three main options for treatment. They are psychotherapy, medication, or a combination of the two. That chapter also briefly described two specialized "procedural" treatments (ECT and Light Therapy) used in less common situations.

Learning about all of these treatments can help you explore your preferences as you prepare to answer question 3.

Question 3. How do I get diagnosed and how do I get the best care?

The recovery process begins when you ask this fundamental question. Not only do you need a correct diagnosis, you also need the kind of care that will give you the best chance for recovering from depression. Depending on your particular situation and circumstances, you may have barriers and obstacles that interfere with your ability to get the best care. This question leads us to Step 4.

Step 4. Evaluating resources and barriers to getting care

The first part of Chapter 4 led you through a process of examining your resources and evaluating any barriers that might interfere with getting an evaluation and ongoing care. Assessing both issues (resources and barriers) is crucial to getting the kind of care that you need.

Step 5. Getting a clinical evaluation and starting treatment

Chapter 4 also addressed the pivotal and most important step: getting the correct diagnosis. After reading the first few chapters of this book, you may reach the conclusion that you or a loved one has Clinical Depression. To begin treatment you need this diagnosis confirmed by a trained professional. This section helped you determine your preferences both for the form of treatment and the type of clinician to provide care.

Question 4. What can I do to help myself?

Along with starting treatment, it is important to do things that promote your health and well-being. Making even modest changes can reap big rewards in terms of helping you feel better.

Step 6. Doing the things that help improve my symptoms

Clinical Depression causes people to feel listless and fatigued. Because of this, even those with mild symptoms can have trouble finding the motivation to take on anything new.

Chapter 5 reviewed 10 of the things that the depressed can do to help themselves. Although they are simple, they require some effort and a commitment to getting well. Each of these things can work together with clinical treatment to ease symptoms.

Question 5. Do I have any special problems that can affect my treatment and recovery?

As you go through the steps toward getting care, you may find that you have special problems or issues that either impact your ability to get care or affect your treatment choices. Although it's important to review these things at the beginning of treatment, it's equally important to keep them in mind as you recover from Clinical Depression. These issues can complicate each stage of this disorder. They require a higher level of attention and care.

Step 7. Determine whether I have any special issues or circumstances

Chapter 6 covered several special issues that can affect the diagnosis and management of Clinical Depression. It started off by briefly exploring the Surgeon General's findings on the impact of race, ethnicity, and culture on the ability to get good quality assessments and treatments. Additionally there were suggestions for how to handle prejudice and discrimination (which can be based on race, ethnicity, gender, age and sexual orientation) when it occurs in medical settings.

Children, adolescents, and the elderly need more complex assessments and treatments. Many of them are more sensitive to medications and their side effects than young to middle-aged adults. Because of these issues, some need treatment with a physician specialist.

Experiencing a life-threatening event can slow the recovery from Clinical Depression. This section discussed the normal phases of emotional adjustment to this kind of trauma.

Other special circumstances that can alter the treatment plan include persistent thoughts about suicide and pregnancy.

Question 6. I've started treatment. How do I live with depression while I heal?

Although the process of recovery begins with your medical assessment, the real healing begins when you start treatment. The process takes time and requires patience. Learning about the stages of recovery is a way to help you chart your progress and alert you when things are not going well.

Step. 8. Learn the stages of recovery

Chapter 7 described the stages of recovery and gave estimates for how long each stage should last. These estimates are only guidelines to help you assess if things are going well. The stages begin with the start of treatment and end when your symptoms resolve.

Sometimes depressed people need to have adjustments made to their schedules and work assignments. They may also need to have a family member take over responsibilities at home. The second part of Chapter 7 turned to work and family issues and suggested ways to talk with loved ones and colleagues about them.

Question 7. How do I stay well?

This chapter started with the statement that recovery is a process, not a single isolated event. The process of healing continues after treatment stops. After getting better, it is still important to pay attention to how you feel and to continue to do the things that promote emotional and physical health.

Part II of this chapter focuses on strategies for staying well. This section is not only for those who are at the stage of terminating treatment. These principles apply to anyone who has ever had a depressive episode.

There are two basic reasons for developing a management plan for staying well. The first is to help you find a way of living that can minimize the risk of having future depressive episodes. The second reason is to give you a systematic way of solving the problems that emerge if you begin to have symptoms again.

PART II. MY PLAN FOR STAYING WELL

A. *Continue to do the things that help you feel better*

One of the early tasks of recovery is to find out what makes you feel better. If you tried some of the things mentioned in Chapter 5, you probably realize by now that putting forth the effort was well worth the gains that you made in relieving some of your symptoms. Of the things mentioned in that chapter, there are six techniques that should be continued throughout the post-recovery period. They are: having a regular bedtime, getting daily moderate exercise, managing stress, not staying alone for long periods, eating a healthy diet, and avoiding addictive substances like alcohol and illegal or recreational drugs. All of these are things that promote physical and emotional health.

B. *Keep in contact with your doctor or therapist*

For those who are no longer in treatment, it is a good idea to keep in contact with your doctor or therapist. That way, if you need help in the future, you can go to someone who knows you and understands your medical history. One of the easiest ways to do this is by having a yearly follow-up visit to assess and confirm your progress. Keep telephone numbers and addresses in a place where you can easily find them.

In the event that either you or your doctor/therapist moves or leaves the area, make sure that you have a back-up person or clinic where you can get care. Keep a list of all medications, including those that didn't work. This information will help guide your future treatment.

C. Strategize ways to overcome barriers to future care

If you need to review possible barriers, you can re-read Chapter 4. To briefly recap, some of the important barriers to getting care are: health insurance status, health insurance plan restrictions, difficulty getting time off from work for office visits, family and/or cultural attitudes that interfere with seeking care, lack of adequate childcare, transportation problems, language, and lack of available healthcare facilities. All of these things can be continuing issues and each of them can be difficult to overcome. Chapter 4 also gives suggestions for ways to minimize and manage obstacles.

D. Getting early treatment for any symptoms that recur

It is important that you continue to pay attention to symptoms, especially those you experienced during your most recent depressive episode. Don't overlook or underestimate symptoms in hopes that they'll just go away. Ignoring your feelings will only prolong the discomfort and put you at risk for developing a more severe form of the illness.

The best predictor of the treatment that will succeed is the treatment that worked in the past. If you took medications, you may be tempted to start yourself on antidepressants by either taking leftover pills or taking a friend's medication. This is a bad idea that can, in fact, be dangerous if it keeps you from getting a good clinical assessment. Also, your age and physical health status may have changed. You need an evaluation to ensure that you get the best and most up-to-date care.

E. Ongoing assessment of how your job and family responsibilities impact how you feel

You may not have the ability to change your responsibilities at work or at home. What you can do, though, is assess your everyday level of stress. Learning relaxation techniques can help you cope until you can modify or change your situation. If stress is a significant problem in your life, ask your doctor for a referral to someone who can help you learn relaxation techniques.

F. When possible, avoid people and things that negatively impact your mood

This may not be possible, especially if these people are family members or colleagues. You can try to limit your contact, though. Associating with people who constantly criticize you or treat you with disrespect is never good. For those with Clinical Depression it can be very damaging because this kind of disapproval can worsen the pessimism and low self-esteem. It is better to nurture supportive relationships, and socialize with those who truly care about you.

After reading the previous section you will probably discover other strategies and techniques to add to your general care plan. These suggestions are meant to be guidelines for you to use. It's important that you customize them to meet your specific needs. Table 8.1 gives you a template to use in constructing your summary plan for recovery.

Table 8.1 Summary of my plan for recovery

My Symptoms (write down the key symptoms you experience with depression):
My Diagnosis:
My Doctors and/or Therapists:
My Health Insurance:
My Medications (names of medications I'm taking):
My Treatment Plan (e.g., type and schedule of medications, schedule of therapy):
Things I can do to help myself:
Things I need to pay attention to (e.g., thoughts, feelings, actions, symptoms, and when I should contact my clinician):

YOU CAN DO IT!

Do you remember the story of Janet Johnson? She's the woman whose story you read in Chapter 1. When we left her she was experiencing severe symptoms and didn't know where to turn. She had little hope of getting better. Fortunately her story didn't end there. Janet's husband became concerned when she started to avoid friends and family members. He noticed that she was no longer interested in her Girl Scout troop and missed several meetings. He finally encouraged her to get a medical evaluation.

She made an appointment with her family doctor. After a complete evaluation and physical her doctor determined that she, indeed, had moderate to severe Clinical Depression. She initially opted for medication management but after a month decided to add psychotherapy to her treatment regimen. Her symptoms resolved over the course of about three months. She continued in treatment for a total of sixteen months.

After the depression her life didn't immediately return to normal. She decided that prior to the onset of symptoms she had taken on too much responsibility at home, at work, and at church. All three had combined to cause her a great deal of stress.

Psychotherapy helped her learn to set priorities and share or delegate tasks. She finally learned that she didn't have to do everything herself. Her therapist also helped her design her plan for staying well.

Janet keeps in touch with both her family doctor and her therapist. She has a yearly appointment with both. Like most who go through a depressive episode, she has been symptom free for years.

Like Janet, you can recover from Clinical Depression. There are many things that you can do to help yourself. You are not doomed to suffer and life is not hopeless. The important thing is to educate yourself about the illness and the treatments so that you can get good care. It is our sincere hope that this book can become a trusted companion on your road to health. You can do it! You can recover from this debilitating illness and live a life of hope and joy.

"When I come across a person that is having similar problems as I had, I always tell them what worked for me. Getting to a good psychologist is most important. Do not stay with a doctor that you feel does not understand you or that you feel is not helping. Always remember that it takes a very long time to start feeling better. Some days you feel up and other days not. Be kind to yourself, do it for yourself."

"What's funny now is that I feel better than I ever did before I got sick. I have made many positive changes in my life and somehow I feel stronger than I was before my depression. Will the depression ever come again? I hope not but I know if it does, I'll be ready for it."

ENDNOTES

Chapter 1

1. *Diagnostic and Statistical Manual of Mental Disorders*, Fourth Edition, Text Revision. Washington, DC, American Psychiatric Association, 2000, p. 326.

Chapter 2

1. O'Donnell, Rosie. To tell the truth. *Rosie, the Magazine* 9 (September 2001):4.
2. Manning, Martha. Home at last. *Rosie, the Magazine* 9 (September 2001):124.
3. Gore, Tipper. Effective service delivery and policy: getting treatments to people and communities. Forum with Tipper Gore at University of California, Los Angeles. Los Angeles, CA: May 7, 1999.
4. Callahan, Michael. Janet's fresh start. *Redbook Magazine* (June 2001):112.
5. Heath, Chris. Blood, Sugar, Sex, Magic. *Rolling Stone* RS872 (July 5, 2001).
6. DSM-IV, pgs. 341–42.

Chapter 3

1. Goldman, Howard H. *Review of General Psychiatry*. 3rd ed. Norwalk/San Mateo: Appleton & Lange, 1992, chapters 33–37.
2. Weissman, M. and Klerman, G. Interpersonal psychotherapy for depression. In: Beitman, B., Klerman, G. eds. *Integrating Pharmacotherapy and Psychotherapy*. Washington, DC: American Psychiatric Press, Inc., 1991: 379–94.
3. Beck, Aaron T., et al. *Cognitive Therapy of Depression*. New York: Guilford Press, 1979.
4. Gabbard, Glen O. Psychoanalysis and psychoanalytic psychotherapy. In Sadock, Benjamin and Virginia Sadock, eds. *Kaplan and Sadock's Comprehensive Textbook of Psychiatry*. 7th ed. Philadelphia: Lippincott Williams and Wilkins, 2000:2076–78.

5. Agency for Health Care Policy and Research. *Depression in Primary Care*. Vol. 2. Washington, DC: U.S. Department of Health and Human Services, 1993.

6. Krishnan, K. Ranga Rama. Monoamine Oxidase Inhibitors. In *American Psychiatric Press Textbook of Psychopharmacology*. 2nd ed. Edited by Alan F. Schatzberg and Charles B. Nemeroff. Washington, DC: American Psychiatric Press, 1998.

7. Belanoff, Joseph K., and Glick, Ira D. New psychotropic drugs for axis I disorders: recently arrived, in development and never arrived. In *American Psychiatric Press Textbook of Psychopharmacology*. 2nd ed. Edited by Alan F. Schatzberg and Charles B. Nemeroff. Washington, DC: American Psychiatric Press, 1998.

8. Linde, Klaus, et al. St. John's wort for depression—An overview and meta-analysis of randomized clinical trials. *British Medical Journal* 313 (1996):256.

9. Agency for Health Care Policy and Research. *Depression in Primary Care*. Vol. 2. Washington, DC: U.S. Department of Health and Human Services, 1993.

10. Fink, Max. How does convulsive therapy work? *Neuropsycopharmacology* 3 (1990):73–82.

11. Isenberg, Keith E. and Charles F. Zorumski. Electroconvulsive therapy. In Sadock, Benjamin and Virginia Sadock, eds. *Kaplan and Sadock's Comprehensive Textbook of Psychiatry*. 7th ed. Philadelphia: Lippincott Williams and Wilkins, 2000:2503–15.

12. Agency for Health Care Policy and Research. *Depression in Primary Care*. Vol. 2. Washington, DC: U.S. Department of Health and Human Services, 1993, p. 150.

13. Kaplan, Harold I. and Benjamin J. Sadock. *Synopsis of Psychiatry: Behavioral Sciences, Clinical Psychiatry*. 8th ed. Baltimore: Lippincott, Williams & Wilkins, 1998.

14. Blehar, M. C. and N. E. Rosenthal. Seasonal affective disorders and phototherapy. Report of a National Institute of Mental Health-sponsored workshop. *Archives of General Psychiatry* 46 (1989):469–74.

15. Agency for Health Care Policy and Research. *Depression in Primary Care*. Vol. 2. Washington, DC: U.S. Department of Health and Human Services, 1993.

16. Keller, M., McCullough, J., Klein, D., Arnow, B. et. al. A comparison of Nefazodone, the cognitive behavioral-analysis system of psychotherapy, and their combination for the treatment of chronic depression. *The New England Journal of Medicine* 342(20) (2000):1462–70.
17. Agency for Health Care Policy and Research. *Depression in Primary Care*. Vol. 2. Washington, DC: U.S. Department of Health and Human Services, 1993, p. 26.
18. Fawcett, J., Scheftner, W., Clark, D., Hedeker, D., Gibbons, R. and Coryell, W. Clinical predictors of suicide in patients with major affective disorders: a controlled prospective study. *American Journal of Psychiatry* 144 (1987):35.

Chapter 4

1. Young, Alexander S., et al. The quality of care for depressive and anxiety disorders in the United States. *Archives of General Psychiatry* 58 (2001):55–61.

Chapter 5

1. Blumenthal, J., Babyak, M., Moore, K., Craighead, W., Herman, S., Khatri, P., Waugh, R., Napolitano, M., Forman, L., Appelbaum, M., Doraiswamy, P. and Krishnan, K. Effects of exercise training on older patients with major depression. *Archives of Internal Medicine* 159(19) 1999:2349–56.
2. Haennel, R. and Lemire, F. Physical activity to prevent cardiovascular disease. How much is enough? *Canadian Family Physician* 48 (2002):65–71.
3. Riise, Trond and Anders Lund. Prognostic factors in major depression: A long-term follow-up of 323 patients. *Journal of Affective Disorders* 65 (2001):305.

Chapter 6

1. Lewontin, R. C. The apportionment of human diversity. *Evolutionary Biology* 6 (1972):381–8.
2. Owens, K. and M. C. King. Genomic views of human history. *Science* 286 (1999):451–53.
3. U.S. Public Health Services. Mental Health: Culture, Race, Ethnicity—A Supplement to *Mental Health. A Report of the Surgeon Gen-*

eral. Washington, DC: U.S. Department of Health and Human Services, 2001.

4. U.S. Public Health Services. (2001). Mental Health: Culture, Race, Ethnicity—A Supplement to *Mental Health. A Report of the Surgeon General-Executive Summary.* Rockville, MD: U.S. Department of Health and Human Services, Public Health Service, Office of the Surgeon General, p. 5.

5. Kübler-Ross, Elisabeth. *On Death and Dying.* New York: Macmillan, 1969.

6. DeWolfe, Deborah J. Responses to Disaster. In *Training Manual for Mental Health and Human Service Workers in Major Disasters.* 2nd ed. Edited by Diana Nordboe. Department of Health and Human Services, Substance Abuse and Mental Health Services Administration, Center for Mental Health Services. DHHS Pub No. ADM 90-538 (2000):5–16.

7. Kübler-Ross, 1969.

8. Pataki, Caroly S. Mood disorders and suicide in children and adolescents. In Sadock, Benjamin and Virginia Sadock, eds. *Kaplan and Sadock's Comprehensive Textbook of Psychiatry.* 7th ed. Philadelphia: Lippincott Williams and Wilkins, 2000:2740–57.

9. Litman, R. E., et al. Prediction models of suicidal behaviors. In *The Prediction of Suicide*, edited by H. Beck, L. P. Resnik, and D. J. Lettieri. Bowie: Charles Press, 1974.

Chapter 7

1. Frank, E., et al. Conceptualization and rationale for consensus definitions of terms in major depressive disorder: Response, remission, recovery, relapse and recurrence. *Archives of General Psychiatry* 48 (1991):852–53.

2. Agency for Health Care Policy and Research. *Depression in Primary Care.* Vol. 2. Washington, DC: U.S. Department of Health and Human Services, 1993, p. 116.

3. Ibid, pgs. 110–112.

4. Ibid.

REFERENCES

Agency for Health Care Policy and Research. *Depression in Primary Care.* Vol. 2. Washington, DC: U.S. Department of Health and Human Services, 1993.

American Psychiatric Association. Practice guidelines for major depressive disorder in adults. *American Journal of Psychiatry* 150 (1993):S1–26.

Asarnow, J., Jaycox, L., and Tompson, M. Depression in youth: psychosocial interventions. *Journal of Clinical Child Psychology* 30(1) (2001):33–47.

Beardslee, William R. and Tracy R. G. Gladstone. Prevention of childhood depression. *Biological Psychiatry* 49 (2001):1101–10.

Beck, A., and Freeman, A. *Cognitive Therapy of Personality Disorders.* New York: The Guilford Press, 1990.

Beck, Aaron T., et al. *Cognitive Therapy of Depression.* New York: Guilford Press, 1979.

Belanoff, Joseph K., and Glick, Ira D. New psychotropic drugs for axis I disorders: recently arrived, in development and never arrived. In *American Psychiatric Press Textbook of Psychopharmacology.* 2nd ed. Edited by Alan F. Schatzberg and Charles B. Nemeroff. Washington, DC: American Psychiatric Press, 1998.

Blazer, D., Kessler, R., McGonagle, K., and Swartz, M. The prevalence and distribution of major depression in a national community sample: The national comorbidity study. *American Journal of Psychiatry* 151(7) (1994):979–86.

Blehar, M. C. and N. E. Rosenthal. Seasonal affective disorders and phototherapy. Report of a National Institute of Mental Health-sponsored workshop. *Archives of General Psychiatry* 46 (1989):469–74.

REFERENCES

Blumenthal, J., Babyak, M., Moore, K., Craighead, W., Herman, S., Khatri, P., Waugh, R., Napolitano, M., Forman, L., Appelbaum, M., Doraiswamy, P. and Krishnan, K. Effects of exercise training on older patients with major depression. *Archives of Internal Medicine* 159(19) 1999:2349–56.

Bruce, M. and Hoff, R. Social and physical health risk factors for first onset major depressive disorder in a community sample. *Social Psychiatry and Psychiatric Epidemiology* 29 (1994):165–71.

Callahan, Michael. Janet's fresh start. *Redbook Magazine* (June 2001).

Carter, Rosalynn with Golant, Susan. *Helping Someone with Mental Illness.* New York: Times Books, 1998.

Coulehan, J., Schulberg, H., Block, M., Janosky, J. and Arena, V. Medical comorbidity of major depressive disorder in a primary medical practice. *Archives of Internal Medicine* 150 (1990):2363–67.

DeWolfe, Deborah J. Responses to Disaster. In *Training Manual for Mental Health and Human Service Workers in Major Disasters.* 2nd ed. Edited by Diana Nordboe. Department of Health and Human Services, Substance Abuse and Mental Health Services Administration, Center for Mental Health Services. DHHS Pub No. ADM 90-538 (2000).

Diagnostic and Statistical Manual of Mental Disorders, Fourth Edition, Text Revision. Washington, DC, American Psychiatric Association, 2000, p. 326.

Druss, B., Rohrbaugh, R., and Rosenheck, R. Depressive symptoms and health costs in older medical patients. *American Journal of Psychiatry* 156(3) (1999):477–79.

Ettner, S., Frank, R., and Kessler, R. The impact of psychiatric disorder on labor market outcomes. *Industrial and Labor Relations Review* 51(1) (1997):64–81.

Fawcett, J., Scheftner, W., Clark, D., Hedeker, D., Gibbons, R. and Coryell, W. Clinical predictors of suicide in patients with major affective disorders: a controlled prospective study. *American Journal of Psychiatry* 144 (1987):35–40.

Fink, Max. How does convulsive therapy work? *Neuropsychopharmacology* 3 (1990):73–82.

Ford, D., Mead, L., Chang, P., Cooper-Patrick, L, Wang, N., and Klag, M. Depression is a risk factor for coronary artery disease in men: the precursors study. *Archives of Internal Medicine* 158(13) (1998):1422–26.

Frank, E., Kupfer, D., Perel, J., Cornes, C., et al. Three-year outcomes for maintenance therapies in recurrent depression. *Archives of General Psychiatry* 47 (12) (1990):1093–99.

Frank, E., et al. Conceptualization and rationale for consensus definitions of terms in major depressive disorder: Response, remission, recovery, relapse and recurrence. *Archives of General Psychiatry* 48 (1991):851–5.

Gitlin, Michael. *The psychotherapist's guide to psychopharmacology.* 2nd ed. New York: Free Press, 1996.

Goldman, Howard H. *Review of General Psychiatry.* 3rd ed. Norwalk/San Mateo: Appleton & Lange, 1992.

Gore, Tipper. Effective service delivery and policy: getting treatments to people and communities. Forum with Tipper Gore at University of California, Los Angeles. Los Angeles, CA: May 7, 1999.

Greenberg, P., Stiglin, L., Finkelstein, S., and Berndt, E. The economic burden of depression in 1990. *Journal of Clinical Psychiatry* 54(11) (1993):405–18.

Haennel, R. and Lemire, F. Physical activity to prevent cardiovascular disease. How much is enough? *Canadian Family Physician* 48 (2002):65–71.

Heath, Chris. Blood, Sugar, Sex, Magic. *Rolling Stone* RS872 (July 5, 2001).

Hunkeler, E., Meresman, J., Hargreaves, W. et al. Efficacy of nurse telehealth care and peer support in augmenting treatment of depression in primary care. *Archives of Family Medicine* 9 (2000):700–708.

Jackson-Triche, M., Sullivan, G., Wells, K., Rogers, W., Camp, P. and Mazel, R. Depression and health-related quality of life in ethnic minorities seeking care in general medical settings. *Journal of Affective Disorders* 58(2) (2000):89–97.

Kaplan, Harold I. and Benjamin J. Sadock. *Synopsis of Psychiatry: Behavioral Sciences, Clinical Psychiatry.* 8th ed. Baltimore: Lippincott Williams & Wilkins, 1998.

Katon, W., Robinson, P., Von Korff, M., Lin, E., Bush, T., Ludman, E., Simon, G., and Walker, E. A multi-faceted intervention to improve treatment of depression in primary care. *Archives of General Psychiatry* 53(10) (1996):924–32.

Katon, W., Von Korff, M., Lin, E., Walker, E., Simon, G., Bush, T. et al. Collaborative management to achieve treatment guidelines: Impact on depression in primary care. *Journal of the American Medical Association* 273 (1995):1026–31.

Katz, S., Kessler, R., Lin, E., and Wells, K. Medication management of depression in the United States and Ontario. *Journal of General Internal Medicine* 13(2) (1998):77–85.

Kelleher, J. and Long, N. Barriers and new directions in mental health services research in the primary care setting. *Journal of Clinical Child Psychology* 23(2) (1994):133–42.

Keller, M., McCullough, J., Klein, D., Arnow, B. et al. A Comparison of Nefazodone, the cognitive behavioral-analysis system of psychotherapy, and their combination for the treatment of chronic depression. *The New England Journal of Medicine* 342(20) (2000):1462–70.

Kessler, R., McGonagle, K., Zhao, S., Nelson, C., Hughes, M., Eshleman, S. et al. Lifetime and 12-month prevalence of DSM-III-R psychiatric disorders in the United States: Results from the National Comorbidity Study. *Archives of General Psychiatry* 51(1) (1994):8–19.

Kohn, Linda T., Corrigan, Janet M., and Molla S. Donaldson, Editors; Committee on Quality of Health Care in America, Institute of Medicine. *To Err Is Human: Building a Safer Health System.* Washington, DC: National Academy Press, 2000.

Krishnan, K. Ranga Rama. Monoamine oxidase inhibitors. In *American Psychiatric Press Textbook of Psychopharmacology.* 2nd ed. Edited by Alan F. Schatzberg and Charles B. Nemeroff. Washington, DC: American Psychiatric Press, 1998.

Kübler-Ross, Elisabeth. *On Death and Dying.* New York: Macmillan, 1969.

Lave, J., Frank, R., Schulberg, H.C. et al. Cost-effectiveness of treatments for major depression in primary care practice. *Archives of General Psychiatry* 55 (1998):645–51.

Lawson, W.B. Clinical issues in the pharmacotherapy of African-Americans. *Psychopharmacology Bulletin* 32 (1986):275–81.

Lenert, L., Sherbourne, C., Sugar, C. et al. Estimation of utilities for the effects of depression from the SF-12. *Medical Care* 38 (2000):763–70.

Lewinsolm, P., Munoz, R., Youngren, M., and Zeiss, A. *Control Your Depression.* New York, NY: Prentice Hall Press, 1986.

Lewontin, R. C. The apportionment of human diversity. *Evolutionary Biology* 6 (1972):381–8.

Lin, E., Katon, W., Simon, G., Von Korff, M., Bush, T., Rutter, C. et al. Achieving guidelines for the treatment of depression in primary care: Is physician education enough? *Medical Care* 35(8) (1997):831–42.

Linde, Klaus, et al. St. John's wort for depression—An overview and meta-analysis of randomized clinical trials. *British Medical Journal* 313 (1996):253–8.

Litman, R. E., et al. Prediction models of suicidal behaviors. In *The Prediction of Suicide*, edited by H. Beck, L. P. Resnik, and D. J. Lettieri. Bowie: Charles Press, 1974.

Ludman, E., Von Korff, M., Katon, W., Lin, E., Simon, G., Walker, E., Unutzer, J., Bush, T. and Wahab, S. The design, implementation, and acceptance of a primary care-based intervention to prevent depression relapse. *International Journal of Psychiatry Medicine* 30(3) (2000):229–45.

Manning, Martha. Home at last. *Rosie, the Magazine* 9 (2001):124

Meredith, L., Jackson-Triche, M., Duan, N., Rubenstein, L., Camp, P., and Wells, K. Quality improvement for depression enhances long-term treatment knowledge for primary care clinicians. *Journal of General Internal Medicine*15(12) (2000):868–77.

Mintz, J., Mintz, L., Arruda, M., and Hwang, S. Treatments of depression and the functional capacity to work. *Archives of General Psychiatry* 49 (1992):761–68.

Miranda, J. and Munoz, R. Intervention for minor depression in primary care patients. *Psychosomatic Medicine* 56 (1994) 136–42.

Moore, R. Improving the treatment of depression in primary care: problems and prospects. *British Journal of General Practice* 47(422) (1997):587–90.

Muñoz, R., and Miranda, J. Group Therapy of Cognitive Behavioral Treatment of Depression, San Francisco General Hospital Depression Clinic, 1986. Santa Monica, CA: RAND; 2000. Document MR-1198/4.

Muñoz, R., Aguilar-Gaxiola, S., and Guzmán, J. Manual de Terapia de Grupo para el Tratamiento Cognitivo-conductal de Depresión, Hospital General de San Francisco, Clínica de Depresión, 1986. Santa Monica, CA: RAND; 2000. Document MR-1198/5.

Murray, C. and Lopez, A. *The Global Burden of Disease: A Comprehensive Assessment of Mortality and Disability from Disease, Injuries, and Risk Factors in 1990 and Projected to 2020.* Boston, MA: The Harvard School of Public Health on behalf of the World Health Organization and The World Bank, 1996.

Narrow, W., Rae, D., Moscicki, E., Locke, B., and Regier, D. Depression among Cuban Americans: The Hispanic health and nutrition examination survey. *Social Psychiatry and Psychiatric Epidemiology* 25(5) (1990):260–68.

National Depressive and Manic Depressive Association. *Beyond Diagnosis: A Landmark Survey of Patients, Partners and Health Profes-*

sionals on Depression and Treatment. Chicago, IL: National DMDA, 2000.

NIMH Consensus Development Conference Statement. Mood disorders: Pharmacologic prevention of recurrences. *American Journal of Psychiatry* 142 (1985):469–76.

O'Donnell, Rosie. To tell the truth. *Rosie, the Magazine* 9 (Sept. 2001).

Olfson, M., Zarin, D., Mittman, B., and McIntyre, J. Is gender a factor in psychiatrists' evaluation and treatment of patients with major depression? *Journal of Affective Disorders* 63(1-3) (2001):149-57.

Owens, K. and M. C. King. Genomic views of human history. *Science* 286 (1999):451–53.

Oxford English Dictionary. Ed. J.A. Simpson and E.S.C. Weiner. 2nd ed. Oxford: Clarendon Press, 1989. OED online.http://oed.com

Radloff, L. The CES-D Scale: a self-report depression scale for research in the general population. *Applied Psychological Measurement* 1 (1977):385–401.

Rao, U., Ryan, N., Birmaher, B., Dahl, R., Williamson, D., Kaufman, J. et al. Unipolar depression in adolescents: Clinical outcome in adulthood. *Journal of the American Academy of Child and Adolescent Psychiatry* 34(5) (1995):566–78.

Regier, D., Narrow, W., Rae, D., Manderscheid, R., Locke, B. and Goodwin, F. The de facto US mental and addictive disorders service system: Epidemiologic catchment area prospective 1-year prevalence rates of disorders and services. *Archives of General Psychiatry* 50(2) (1993):85–94.

Riise, Trond and Anders Lund. Prognostic factors in major depression: A long-term follow-up of 323 patients. *Journal of Affective Disorders* 65 (2001):297–306.

Robins, L. and Regier, D. *Psychiatric Disorders in America. The Epidemiologic Catchment Area Study.* New York: The Free Press, 1991.

Rost, K., Fortney, J., Zhang, M., Smith, J., and Smith, G. Treatment of depression in rural Arkansas: Policy implications for improving care. *Journal of Rural Health* 15 (1999):308–15.

Rost, Kathryn, Audrey Burnam, and R. Smith. Development of screeners for depressive disorders and substance disorder history. *Medical Care* 31 (1993):189–200.

Rubenstein, L., Jackson-Triche, M., Minnium, K., Unutzer, J., Miranda, J., Mulrow, C. and Wells, K. *Are You Feeling...Tired, Sad, Angry, Irritable, Hopeless?* Santa Monica: RAND, 2000.

Rubenstein, L., Jackson-Triche, M., Unützer, J., Miranda, J., Minnium, K., Pearson, M. and Wells, K. Evidence-based care for depression in managed primary care practices. *Health Affairs* 18(5) (1999):89–105.

Rubenstein, L., Unutzer, J., Minnium, K., Wells, K. and Klein, C. *Guidelines for the Study Therapist.* Santa Monica: RAND, 2000.

Rubenstein, L., Unutzer, J., Miranda, J., Katon, W., Wieland, M., Jackson-Triche, J., Minnium, K., Mulrow, C. and Wells, K. *Clinician Guide to Depression Assessment and Management in Primary Care Settings.* Santa Monica: RAND, 2000.

Rubenstein, L., Unutzer, J., Miranda, J., Simon, B., Katon, W., Jackson-Triche, J., Minnium, K. and Wells, K. *Guidelines and Resources for the Depression Nurse Specialist.* Santa Monica: RAND, 2000.

Ryan, N., Puig-Antich, J., Ambrosini, P., Rabinovich, H., Robinson, D., Nelson, B. et al. The clinical picture of major depression in children and adolescents. *Archives of General Psychiatry* 44(10) (1987):854–61.

Sadock, Benjamin and Virginia Sadock, eds. *Kaplan and Sadock's Comprehensive Textbook of Psychiatry.* 7th ed. Philadelphia: Lippincott Williams and Wilkins, 2000.

Schatzberg, Alan F. and Charles B. Nemeroff. *American Psychiatric Press Textbook of Psychopharmacology.* 2nd ed. Washington, DC: American Psychiatric Press, 1998.

Schoenbaum, M., Unützer, J., Sherbourne, C., Duan, N., Rubenstein, L., Miranda, J., Meredith, L., Carney, M. and Wells, K. Cost-effectiveness of practice-initiated quality improvement for depression: Results of a randomized controlled trial. *Journal of the American Medical Association* 286(11) (2001):1325–30.

Schulberg, H.C., Block, M., Madonia, M. et al. Treating major depression in primary care practice: 8-month clinical outcomes. *Archives of General Psychiatry* 53 (1996):913–19.

Schuster MA, Stein BD, Jaycox LH, Collins RL, Marshall GN, Elliott MN, Zhou AJ, Kanouse DE, Morrison JL, Berry SH. A National Survey of Stress Reactions after the September 11, 2001, Terrorist Attacks. *New England Journal of Medicine*, Vol.345, No. 20, November 15, 2001, pp. 1507–12.

Sherbourne, C., Dwight-Johnson, M. and Klap, R. Psychological distress, unmet need, and barriers to mental health care for women. *Womens Health Issues* 11(3) (2001):231–43.

Sherbourne, C., Sturm, R. and Wells, K. What outcomes matter to patients? A study of patient preferences in primary care. *Journal of General Internal Medicine* 14(6) (1999):357–64.

Sherbourne, C., Wells, K., Duan, N., Miranda, J., Unützer, J., Jaycox, L., Schoenbaum, M., Meredith, L. and Rubenstein, L. Long-term effectiveness of disseminating quality improvement for depression in primary care. *Archives of General Psychiatry* 58(7) (2001):696–703.

Simon, G. and Ludman, E. Lessons from recent research on depression in primary care. *Epidemiologia e Psichiatria Sociale II Pensiero Scientifico Editore*: Italy 9(3) (2001):145–51.

Simon, G., Manning, W., Katzelnick, D., Pearson, S., Henk, H. and Helstad, C. Cost-effectiveness of systematic depression treatment for high utilizers of general medical care. *Archives of General Psychiatry* 58(2) (2001):181–87.

Simon, G., Von Korff, M., Rutter, C. and Wagner, E. Randomized trial of monitoring, feedback, and management of care by telephone to improve treatment of depression in primary care. *British Medical Journal* 320(7234) (2000):550–54.

Sirey, J., Bruce, M., Alexopoulos, G., Perlick, D., Raue, P., Friedman, S. and Meyers, B. Perceived stigma as a predictor of treatment discontinuation in young and older outpatients with depression. *American Journal of Psychiatry* 158 (2001):479–81.

Solomon, Andrew. *The Noonday Demon: An Atlas of Depression.* New York: Scribner, 2001.

Sturm, R. and Wells, K. How can care for depression become more cost-effective? *Journal of the American Medical Association* 273(1) (1995):51–58.

Sturm, R. and Wells, K. Health insurance may be improving – but not for individuals with mental illness. *Health Services Research* 35 (2000):253–62.

Styron, William. *Darkness Visible: a memoir of madness.* New York: Random House, 1990.

Sussman, L., Robins, L. and Earls, F. Treatment-seeking for depression by black and white Americans. *Social Science and Medicine* 24 (1987):187–96.

Takeuchi, D., Chung, R., Lin, K., Shen, H., Kurasaki, K., Chun, C., and Sue, S. Lifetime and twelve-month prevalence rates of major depressive episodes and dysthymia among Chinese Americans in Los Angeles. *American Journal of Psychiatry* 155(10) (1998):1407–14.

Unützer, J., Rubenstein, L., Katon, W., Tang, L., Duan, N., Lagomasino, I. and Wells, K. Two-year effects of quality improvement programs on medication management for depression. *Archives of General Psychiatry* 58(10) (2001):935–42.

U.S. Department of Health and Human Services. *Mental Health: A Report of the Surgeon General.* Rockville, MD: US Department of Health and Human Services Administration, Center for Mental Health Services, National Institutes of Health, National Institute of Mental Health, 1999.

U.S. Public Health Services. Mental Health: Culture, Race, Ethnicity— A Supplement to *Mental Health. A Report of the Surgeon General.* Washington, DC: U.S. Department of Health and Human Services, 2001.

U.S. Public Health Services. (2001). Mental Health: Culture, Race, Ethnicity—A Supplement to *Mental Health. A Report of the Surgeon*

General-Executive Summary. Rockville, MD: U.S. Department of Health and Human Services, Public Health Service, Office of the Surgeon General.

Unützer, J., Katon, W., Williams, J.W. Jr., Callahan, C., Harpole, L., Hunkeler, E., Hoffing, M., Arean, P., Hegel, M., Schoenbaum, M., Oishi, S. and Langston, C. Improving primary care for depression in late life: the design of a multicenter randomized trial. *Medical Care* 39(8) (2001):785–99.

Unützer, J., Patrick, D., Simon, G., Grembowski, D., Walker, E., Rutter, C. and Katon, W. Depressive symptoms and the cost of health services in HMO patients aged 65 years and older. A 4-year prospective study. *Journal of the American Medical Association* 277(20) (1997):1618–23.

Vega, W., Kolody, B., Aguilar-Gaxiola, S., Alderete, E., Catalano, R., and Caraveo-Anduaga, J. Lifetime prevalence of DSM-III-R psychiatric disorders among urban and rural Mexican Americans in California. *Archives of General Psychiatry* 55 (1998): 771–78.

Von Korff, M., Katon, W., Bush, T., Lin, E., Simon, G., Saunders, K., Ludman, E., Walker, E. and Unützer, J. Treatment costs, cost offset, and cost-effectiveness of collaborative management of depression. *Psychosomatic Medicine* 60(2) (1998):143–49.

Wang, P., Berglund, P. and Kessler, R. Recent care of common mental disorders in the United States: Prevalence and conformance with evidence-based recommendations. *Journal of General Internal Medicine* 15(5) (2000):284–92.

Weissman, M. and Klerman, G. Interpersonal psychotherapy for depression. In: Beitman, B., Klerman, G. eds. *Integrating Pharmacotherapy and Psychotherapy.* Washington, DC: American Psychiatric Press, Inc., 1991: 379–94.

Weissman, Myrna and Klerman G., Psychotherapy with depressed women: An empirical study of content themes and reflection. *Br J Psychiatry* 123 (1973):55.

Wells, K., Kataoka, S. and Asarnow, J. Affective disorders in children and adolescents: addressing unmet need in primary care settings. *Biological Psychiatry* 49(12) (2001):1111–20.

Wells, K., Schoenbaum, M., Unützer, J., Lagomasino, I. and Rubenstein, L. Quality of care for depressed primary care patients. *Archives of Family Medicine* 8 (1999):529–36.

Wells, K. and Sherbourne, C. Functioning and utility for depression compared to chronic medical conditions in primary care, managed care patients. *Archives of General Psychiatry* 56(10) (1999):897–904.

Wells, K., Sherbourne, C., Schoenbaum, M., Duan, N., Meredith, L., Unützer, J., Miranda, J., Carney, M. and Rubenstein, L. 2000. Impact of disseminating quality improvement programs for depression in primary care: a randomized controlled trial. *Journal of the American Medical Association* 283(2) (2000):212–20.

Wells, K., Sturm, R., Sherbourne, C. and Meredith, L. *Caring for Depression.* Cambridge: Harvard University Press, 1996.

Wells, Kenneth B. The design of Partners in Care: Evaluating the cost effectiveness of improving care for depression in primary care. *Social Psychiatry and Psychiatric Epidemiology* 34 (1999):20–9.

Young, Alexander S., et al. The quality of care for depressive and anxiety disorders in the United States. *Archives of General Psychiatry* 58 (2001):55–61.

GLOSSARY

Addiction. Habitual drive for and use of substances, such as alcohol, drugs or tobacco, with harmful consequences for the individual and/or their loved ones.

Adjustment disorders. Illness that develops as a reaction to a difficult life event. Symptoms are less severe than in Clinical Depression and the disorder will usually get better within six months of the event.

Affective Disorder. The large class of mood disorders that includes Clinical Depression and mania or Bipolar Disorder.

Bipolar disorder (also known as *Manic Depression*). Mood disorder that causes periods of extreme highs (mania) and extreme lows (depression).

Clinical Depression. A severe form of depression affecting mood with several other types of symptoms or problems at the same time, and lasting at least two weeks but commonly several months or years. Includes Major Depression, Dysthymic Disorder, and Seasonal Affective Disorder.

Clinical evaluation. Assessment of a person's health, well-being, and functioning.

Clinician. Healthcare professional who provides treatment; e.g., doctor, therapist, psychologist, psychiatrist.

Cognitive behavioral therapy. Type of therapy for mental, emotional, and behavioral health problems. Focuses on identifying and changing the individual's thoughts, actions, and feelings that contribute to the problem.

Cyclic antidepressants. Type of prescription medication used to treat mental, emotional, and behavioral health problems, mainly depression. Tricyclic antidepressants are one class of cyclic antidepressants.

Depression. A disturbance of affect or mood with associated symptoms such as poor sleep, appetite, or physical problems. Includes minor symptoms as well as different forms of Clinical Depression.

Dysthymic disorder. Type of Clinical Depression that is characterized by recurring episodes of depression over a period of at least two years. Symptoms may not be as severe as in Major Depressive Disorder.

Electroconvulsive therapy. Treatment for mental health disorders (administered by a psychiatrist) that delivers low-voltage current through electrodes attached to the patient, while the patient is under anesthesia. Highly effective for severe depression.

Functioning. Describes a person's perceptions of their health and their ability to carry out their daily activities.

Herbals. Preparations of herbs available over-the-counter. Some herbals have been promoted as a treatment for depression, their effectiveness is not yet known.

Initiation of treatment. Start of a treatment episode.

Inpatient care. Treatment for a health problem received while in a hospital or other overnight healthcare facility.

Insurance status. Indicates whether a person has health insurance and, if so, what type.

Interpersonal therapy. Form of therapy used to treat mental, emotional, and behavioral problems. Focuses on identifying and coping better with the events, people, or circumstances that cause or worsen the emotional problems.

Licensed Clinical Social Worker (Social Worker) (L.C.S.W.). Mental health professional who treats mental, emotional, and behavioral health problems with therapeutic techniques.

Light therapy. Treatment used for seasonal affective disorder, in which the patient is exposed to exceptionally bright artificial light, prescribed by a physician.

Maintenance treatment. Continuing treatment (usually medication) after recovery to avoid subsequent episodes of Clinical Depression.

Major Depressive Disorder. Type of Clinical Depression that is characterized by mood disturbance and the presence of multiple symptoms of depression, occurring daily for two weeks or more and usually lasting several months.

Mania. A type of Bipolar Disorder that dramatically affects an individual's feelings, thoughts, and behaviors, and causes them to be very agitated, hyperactive, and euphoric.

Marriage and family therapist (M.F.T.) [also known as marriage, family, and child counselor (M.F.C.C.)]. Mental health professional who treats mental, emotional, and behavioral problems with therapy.

Minor Depression. Presence of symptoms of depression that are either less severe or do not last long enough to meet criteria for Major Depressive Disorder or Dysthymic Disorder.

Monoamine oxidase inhibitor. Type of medication used to treat depression.

Neurotransmitters. Chemicals in the brain that carry messages between brain cells.

Norepinephrine. One of the neurotransmitters in the brain that regulates mood.

Outpatient care (also known as *day treatment*). Treatment for a health problem provided at a healthcare facility that does not require the patient to stay overnight.

Posttraumatic stress disorder. Illness that develops as a result of experiencing or witnessing life-threatening and/or violent events or attacks.

Psychiatrist (M.D.). Medical doctor who specializes in mental, emotional, and behavioral disorders. Conducts evaluations and provides treatment, using therapy, medication, electroconvulsive therapy, and/or light therapy.

Psychodynamic therapy. Form of treatment for mental, emotional, and behavioral health problems that focuses on identifying and resolving emotional conflicts that arise from the interaction between personality and circumstance.

Psychologist (Ph.D.). Doctoral-level mental health professional trained in evaluating and treating mental, emotional, and behavioral health problems through the use of therapy and other treatments.

Psychosis. A form of severe mental illness, in which a person's perception of reality is markedly distorted, affecting their thoughts, actions, ability to relate to others, and sometimes their ability to care for them or others.

Psychotherapist (also known as *therapist*). Trained mental health professional who evaluates and treats mental, emotional, and behavioral problems, using verbal and nonverbal therapeutic techniques.

Psychotherapy (also known as *therapy*). Treatment for mental, emotional, and behavioral problems that involves talking to a trained health professional.

Recurrence (relapse). A new episode of an illness after a period of remission.

Remission. Recovery from an episode of an illness.

Response to treatment. Indicates how the patient is reacting to the treatment.

Seasonal pattern depression (also known as *Seasonal affective disorder*). Depressive disorder that occurs at certain times of the year, typically during the fall or winter months. More common in climates that have long hours of darkness.

Selective serotonin reuptake inhibitors. Type of antidepressant that is used to treat depression and other mood disorders. Thought to elevate mood by increasing the amount of serotonin available to the brain.

Serotonin. One of the neurotransmitters in the brain that regulates mood.

Supportive therapy. Form of treatment for mental, emotional, and behavioral disorders that focuses on helping people deal with the impact of their disorder on their daily life. Not known to be effective when used alone for treating Clinical Depression.

Termination of treatment. Ending or stopping treatment.

Tricyclic antidepressants. A type of cyclic antidepressant.

DEPRESSION
RESOURCES

Advocacy, Support, and Educational Associations or Groups for Patients and Families

Freedom From Fear: Building Bridges from Education to Treatment

Freedom From Fear
308 Seaview Avenue
Staten Island, New York 10305
Phone: (718) 351-1717
Fax: (718) 667-8893
www.freedomfromfear.org

National Alliance for the Mentally Ill (NAMI)

Colonial Place Three
2107 Wilson Blvd., Suite 300
Arlington, VA 22201
Phone: (703) 524-7600
NAMI HelpLine: 1-800-950-NAMI [6264]
www.nami.org

National Depressive and Manic-Depressive Association (NDMDA)

730 N. Franklin Street, Suite 501
Chicago, Illinois 60610-7204
Phone: (800) 826-3632; (312) 642-0049
Fax: (312) 642-7243
www.ndmda.org

National Mental Health Association
1021 Prince Street
Alexandria, VA 22314-2971
Phone: (703) 684-7722
Fax: (703) 684-5968
Mental Health Information Center (800) 969-NMHA
TTY Line (800) 433-5959
www.nmha.org

Scientific and Professional Associations

American Psychiatric Association
1400 K Street N.W.
Washington, DC 20005
Phone: (888) 357-7924
Fax: (202) 682-6850
www.psych.org

American Psychological Association
750 First Street, NE,
Washington, DC 20002-4242
Phone: (800) 374-2721; (202) 336-5510TDD/TTY: (202) 336-6123
www.apa.org

Government Resources

Center for Mental Health Services (CMHS)
Phone: (310) 443-0001
Fax: (310) 443-1563
http://www.samhsa.gov/centers/cmhs/cmhs.html

Center for Nutrition Policy and Promotion (CNPP) (part of the United States Department of Agriculture [USDA])
3101 Park Center Drive, Room 1034
Alexandria, VA 22302-1594

Phone: 703-305-7600
Fax: 703-305-3400
website: www.usda.gov/cnpp

Center for Substance Abuse Prevention (CSAP)
Phone: (310) 443-0365
Fax: (310) 443-5447
http://www.samhsa.gov/centers/csap/csap.html

Center for Substance Abuse Treatment (CSAT)
Phone: (310) 443-5700
Fax: (310) 443-8751
http://www.samhsa.gov/centers/csat/csat.html

Centers for Disease Control and Prevention (CDC)
1600 Clifton Road
Atlanta, GA 30333
Phone: (404) 639-3311
Public Inquiries: (404) 639-3534; (800) 311-3435
http://www.cdc.gov/netinfo.htm
www.cdc.gov

Food and Nutrition Information Center
Agricultural Research Service, USDA
National Agricultural Library, Room 105
10301 Baltimore Avenue
Beltsville, MD 20705-2351
Phone: 301-504-5719
Fax: 301-504-6409
TTY: 301-504-6856
email: fnic@nal.usda.gov
website: http://www.nal.usda.gov/fnic/

Knowledge Exchange Network (KEN)

KEN provides information about mental health through the internet and a toll-free number and offers educational publications.
Phone: (800) 789-2647
TDD: (301) 443-9006
email: ken@mentalhealth.org
www.mentalhealth.org

National Institute of Mental Health (NIMH)

(Part of the National Institutes of Health, which is an agency of the U.S. Department of Health and Human Services)
NIMH Public Inquiries
6001 Executive Boulevard, Rm. 8184, MSC 9663
Bethesda, MD 20892-9663
Phone: (301) 443-4513
Fax: (301) 443-4279
www.nimh.nih.gov

Office of Applied Statistics

Phone: (310) 443-6239
Fax: (310) 443-9847

Office of Communications

Phone: (310) 443-8956
Fax: (310) 443-9050

Office of Managed Care

Phone: (310) 443-2817
Fax: (310) 443-8711

Office of Minority Health

Phone: (310) 443-7265
Fax: (310) 443-9538

Office of Policy and Program Coordination
Phone: (310) 443-4111
Fax: (310) 443-0496

Office of Program Service
Phone: (310) 443-3875
Fax: (310) 443-0247

Office of the Surgeon General
The Surgeon General
Office of the Surgeon General
5600 Fishers Lane
Room 18-66
Rockville, MD 20857
http://www.osophs.dhhs.gov/

Substance Abuse and Mental Health Services Agency (SAMHSA)
(An agency of the U.S. Department of Health and Human Services)
SAMHSA
5600 Fishers Lane
Rockville, MD 20857
www.samhsa.gov

DEPRESSION TOOLKIT

In this book, we have discussed many aspects of depression and we have presented a lot of information. Getting an overall picture of depression is helpful, but the way people experience depression and the special issues they deal with are all very personal. Because depression is so personal, it is important to identify what information is most helpful to you. In order to help you think about your own experience, we have included the following tables, or tools. These are intended to help you better understand what you are experiencing and to help you develop a plan for your road to recovery.

Things I'm experiencing

(Place a check by the symptoms you are experiencing or have experienced in the past few months, then indicate how much that symptom is affecting you.)

✔	Key Symptoms and Problems	Does this symptom affect you a little of the time, some of the time or a lot of the time?
	Feeling sad or "empty"	_____A little ___Some ___A lot
	Loss of interest in things that used to be enjoyable like sex, sports, reading, or listening to music	_____A little ___Some ___A lot
	Trouble concentrating, thinking, remembering, or making decisions	_____A little ___Some ___A lot
	Trouble sleeping or sleeping too much	_____A little ___Some ___A lot

Things I'm experiencing (Cont.)

✔	Key Symptoms and Problems	Does this symptom affect you a little of the time, some of the time or a lot of the time?		
	Loss of energy or feeling tired	____A little	___Some	___A lot
	Loss of appetite or eating too much	____A little	___Some	___A lot
	Losing weight or gaining weight without trying	____A little	___Some	___A lot
	Crying or feeling like crying	____A little	___Some	___A lot
	Feeling irritable or "on edge"	____A little	___Some	___A lot
	Feeling worthless or guilty	____A little	___Some	___A lot
	Feeling hopeless or negative	____A little	___Some	___A lot
	Thinking about death, including thoughts about suicide	____A little	___Some	___A lot
	Frequent headaches, body aches, and pains	____A little	___Some	___A lot
	Stomach and digestive trouble with bowel irregularity	____A little	___Some	___A lot
	Other symptoms:	____A little	___Some	___A lot
		____A little	___Some	___A lot
		____A little	___Some	___A lot

Life events I have experienced: During the past 12 months, did any of the following things happen to you?

Someone close to me died.	YES	NO
I had a serious argument with someone who lives at my home.	YES	NO
I had a serious problem with a close friend, relative, or neighbor not living at home.	YES	NO
I separated, divorced or ended an engagement or relationship.	YES	NO
I had arguments or other difficulties with people at work.	YES	NO
Someone moved out of my home.	YES	NO
I was laid off or fired from work.	YES	NO
I had a serious injury or illness.	YES	NO
I had minor financial problems.	YES	NO
I had a major financial crisis.	YES	NO
Someone close to me had a sudden serious illness or injury.	YES	NO
I, or someone important to me, had problems because of discrimination based on age, gender, race, ethnicity or immigration status?	YES	NO
I lost my home.	YES	NO
Other:	YES	NO

Is alcohol a special problem for me? A "yes" answer to any one of these questions may indicate that you have a drinking problem.

In the last month, was there a single day in which you had five or more drinks of beer, wine, or liquor?	YES NO
Did you ever think that you were an excessive drinker?	YES NO
Has there ever been a period of two weeks when you were drinking seven or more alcoholic drinks (beer, wine, or other alcoholic beverage) a day?	YES NO
Have you ever drunk as much as a fifth of liquor in one day? (That would be about twenty drinks or three bottles of wine or as much as three six-packs of beer in one day.)	YES, more than once YES, but only once NO

My Medications

Name of Medication	Dose and Frequency of Medication
1	Dose (daily, weekly, monthly, as needed)
2	
3	
4	
5	
6	
7	
8	
9	
10	

Comparison of treatments

	Psychotherapy	Medications	ECT	Light Therapy
Appropriate for which levels of severity of Clinical Depression	Mild or moderate	All: (mild, moderate or severe)	Severe	Only used for Seasonal Affective Disorder
Cost	The exact cost to the individual depends on insurance status (whether one has health insurance) and the type of health insurance plan			
Type of trained professional who can provide treatment	Therapist (LCSW, MFCC, MFT), Psychologist (PhD), Psychiatrist (MD)	Psychiatrist (MD), Primary care clinician (MD)	Psychiatrist (MD)	Psychiatrist MD)
Frequency of visits	Weekly sessions (sometimes more than once a week)	Daily medication with follow-up appointment intervals of 1-3 months depend-ing on the rate of improvement	Individualized	Individualized
Duration of treatment	Typically 12 weeks to 1 year, but can last longer	Typically 6 months to 1 year, but can last longer	Typically weeks but can last longer	Typically weeks but can last longer
When you'll start feeling better	Responses to treatment vary by individual. See Chapter 6 for more information about the recovery process.			

What things would make it harder for me to get care?

Which of the following reasons would make it difficult for you to get care?

1. I worry about cost.	YES	NO
2. The clinician won't accept my health insurance.	YES	NO
3. My health plan won't pay for my treatment.	YES	NO
4. I can't find where to go for help.	YES	NO
5. I can't get an appointment as soon as I need one.	YES	NO
6. I can't get to the clinician's office when it's open.	YES	NO
7. It takes too long to get to the clinician's office from my house or work.	YES	NO
8. I can't get through on the telephone or leave messages.	YES	NO
9. I don't think I can be helped.	YES	NO
10. I am too embarrassed to discuss my problem with anyone.	YES	NO
11. I am afraid of what others will think of me.	YES	NO
12. I can't get work leave for medical appointments and will lose pay.	YES	NO
13. I need someone to take care of my children.	YES	NO
14. No one speaks my language at the clinician's office.	YES	NO
15. I feel discriminated against because of my age, race, ethnicity, or sexual orientation.	YES	NO

What is my experience with treatment (my treatment history)?

As you and your doctor discuss treatment options, it's important to talk about your past experiences with depression treatment(s), including those of family members. Discuss your experience and your attitudes about treatment with your doctor.

Have you been diagnosed with depression in the past?	YES	NO
If yes, did you receive any form of treatment?	YES	NO
Have you ever taken antidepressant medications?	YES	NO
If yes, were they helpful?	YES	NO
Have any family or friends taken antidepressant medications?	YES	NO
If yes, were they helpful?	YES	NO
Have you ever tried counseling or therapy?	YES	NO
If yes, was it helpful?	YES	NO
Have any family or friends tried counseling or therapy?	YES	NO
If yes, was it helpful?	YES	NO
Are you against taking medications? If yes, why?	YES	NO
Are you against counseling or therapy? If yes, why?	YES	NO

What are my personal depression treatment preferences?*

✔	Options and preferences
	Psychotherapy alone (for those with mild to moderate symptoms only)
	Medication alone (for those with mild, moderate, or severe symptoms)
	Combination treatment—medication and psychotherapy (for those with mild, moderate, or severe symptoms)

*If all are indicated, and available.

Questions for my doctor

It is important to talk with your doctor about your concerns and preferences regarding treatment and about any special issues you may have. The following are some sample questions you might want to use.

Preferences or Concerns	Sample Questions
If your options and preferences include medication alone	"Will you prescribe my antidepressant medications or will you refer me to a psychiatrist?" "When will I start feeling better?" "Our next appointment is scheduled for _____. If I haven't noticed a change by what date, when should I call you?" "If I don't start feeling better by a certain time, what is the next step?" "Are there any other things I should contact you about before our next appointment?" "What side effects might I experience?" "I also take _____ (list other medications). Is it safe to take all of these together? Should I take them at different times of the day?"
If your options and preferences include psychotherapy alone	"If possible, I would like to try psychotherapy before considering medications. I've read about two special therapies for people with Clinical Depression. Are there therapists who can provide these particular treatments?" *(If the answer is "no," you need to decide whether you would still like to pursue psychotherapy alone or in combination with medications.)* "Can you refer me to a therapist? If not, how can I find one?" "Would you like me to follow-up with you after I have started therapy?" "If I don't notice any change after a certain amount of time, should I contact you? What would the next step be?" "Would you like to speak with the therapist once I start treatment?"

Questions for my doctor (Cont.)

Preferences or Concerns	Sample Questions
If your options and preferences include combination treatment	"I would like to try both medication and psychotherapy. Is there a way to arrange for me to get both treatments?"
(Also see questions for medication and psychotherapy alone.)	"Is that arranged through my health plan or do I need to find a therapist outside of the plan?"
	"Is there anyone who can help me find a therapist?"
	"Would you like to speak with my therapist so that both of you can discuss the treatment?"
	"When should I come in for another appointment with you?"
Questions for the therapist	"What can I expect?"
	"How is the therapy going to help my depression?"
	"At a certain point, should I consider going on medication, if I'm not feeling better?"
	"Would you like to speak with my doctor?"
	"Are there things I should be doing on my own?"
	"If things don't seem to be going right, how should I bring it up with you?"

Things I can do to help myself

In addition to getting treatment from a professional, there are things that you can do to help yourself. We discussed many of these techniques in Chapter 5. Think about actions or activities that can help your recovery process. Small things can make a big difference, so you don't need to plan special activities or make big changes. List the things that you can do to help yourself.

Pleasant Activities

(List activities that you find enjoyable, fun, rewarding, meaningful, or motivational; e.g., watching a movie, taking a nature walk, reading.)

1.

2.

3.

4.

5.

Relaxing Activities

(Name some activities that help to soothe or relax you and reduce stress and worries; e.g., taking a bath, meditation, spiritual practice.)

6.

7.

8.

9.

10.

Exercise, Diet, and Sleep

(What can you do to help yourself maintain a healthy diet, get some regular exercise, and get enough sleep?)

11.

12.

13.

14.

15.

Things I can do to help myself (Cont.)

People, Places, Things to Avoid
(Are there things you should stay away from until you are feeling better?)

16.

17.

18.

19.

20.

Other Ideas for Recovery:

Warning signs: Am I becoming depressed again?*

Put a checkmark by the symptoms you experienced before getting treatment. Review this list from time to time to help you notice if you are becoming clinically depressed again.

✔	Symptom	How I feel now. Is it time to seek help again?
	Feeling sad or "empty"	
	Loss of interest in things that used to be enjoyable, like sex, sports, reading, or listening to music	
	Trouble concentrating, thinking, remembering, or making decisions	
	Trouble sleeping or sleeping too much	
	Loss of energy or feeling tired	
	Loss of appetite or eating too much	
	Losing weight or gaining weight without trying	
	Crying or feeling like crying a lot	
	Feeling irritable or "on edge"	
	Feeling worthless or guilty	
	Feeling hopeless or negative	
	Thinking a lot about death, including thoughts about suicide	
	Frequent headaches, body aches, and pains	
	Stomach and digestive trouble with bowel irregularity	
	Other symptoms:	

* If you start experiencing these symptoms again, talk to your doctor.

Summary of my plan for recovery

My Symptoms (Write down the key symptoms you experience with Clinical Depression):

_____

My Diagnosis:

_____

My Doctors and/or Therapists:

_____

My Health Insurance:

_____

My Medications (names of medications I'm taking):

_____

My Treatment Plan (e.g., type and schedule of medications, schedule of therapy):

_____

Things I can do to help myself:

_____

Things I need to pay attention to (e.g., thoughts, feelings, actions, symptoms, and when I should contact my doctor or therapist):

_____

INDEX